P9-BYO-215

THE LATEST
COUNTRY GARDENS

THE LATEST
COUNTRY GARDENS

George Plumptre

THE BODLEY HEAD
LONDON

To Wyndham and Piers

Frontispiece Biddick Hall, County Durham.
Looking along the main axis of the formal garden
with the house in the background.

British Library Cataloguing
in Publication Data
Plumptre, George
The Latest Country Gardens.
1. Gardens —— England —— History ——
20th century
I. Title
712'.6'0942   SB466.G75E5

ISBN 0–370–30786–0

© George Plumptre 1988
Printed and bound in
Great Britain for
The Bodley Head Ltd
32 Bedford Square
London WC1B 3EL
by Butler & Tanner Ltd, Frome and London
set in Palatino
by Wyvern Typesetting Ltd, Bristol
First published 1988

CONTENTS

ACKNOWLEDGEMENTS

First and most important, I would like to thank all of the owners and their gardeners, for not only allowing me to include their gardens in this book, but also for giving me considerable help when I visited them and often supplying further information. The book would never have been possible without their active involvement.

I would like to thank Nigel Nicolson for allowing me to quote from Vita Sackville-West's poem *The Garden*.

The following people also gave me invaluable help in a variety of ways and I am most grateful: John Bright-Holmes, John Brookes, Sir Ilay Campbell, John Codrington, Dame Sylvia Crowe, Michael Graham, Arthur Hellyer, Sir Geoffrey Jellicoe, James Lees-Milne, John Martin Robinson, Hugh Montgomery-Massingberd, Anthony du Gard Pasley, James Russell, Vernon Russell-Smith, John Sales, Anne Scott-James, Graham Stuart Thomas, Tony Venison and Tom Wright. In addition I must thank David Machin and Jill Black at Bodley Head and my agent, Vivienne Schuster.

Other than in the few cases mentioned here, all of the photographs in the book are my own. I would like to thank Lady Scott, Tanya Midgely, Derry Moore and *Country Life* for their help with the photographs on the following pages. Lady Scott: 122, 124, between pages 128–9; Tanya Midgeley: facing page 33, between pages 48–49, facing page 64, facing page 113, facing page 128; Derry Moore: 42, 54, facing page 64, facing page 80; *Country Life*: 19, 35, 36.

George Plumptre,
Rowling,
Autumn 1987.

Yet shall the garden with the state of war
Apply contrast, a miniature endeavour
To hold the graces and the courtesies
Against a horrid wilderness . . .

THE GARDEN by Vita Sackville-West

INTRODUCTION

The aim of this book is to discuss the evolution of British gardens in the decades since the Second World War. Most books which study the history of British gardens close at 1939. If they venture further, it is usually in the form of a postscript or just a few speculative pages; and while books abound that discuss all sorts and sizes of gardens—town gardens, cottage gardens, shrub gardens, National Trust gardens and even ladies' gardens—they tend to treat their subjects in isolation.

It seems opportune, therefore, to attempt a survey of the most recent period, since 1945, and study the underlying factors and influences which have played a part in the appearance and character of gardens. At the same time I will describe a selection of gardens which illustrate my themes and are often important creations in themselves. I am not attempting a comprehensive survey, however. That would tend to make the book unwieldy and perhaps obscure its central thesis through excess of detail.

This book is planned in part as a companion to *The Latest Country Houses* by John Martin Robinson in which the author discusses and describes those country houses which have been built since the Second World War. Gardens do not fall into such distinct groups, however; large country gardens have strong connections with cottage gardens and town gardens in a way that is not true of houses. None the less, by concentrating on the category which Gertrude Jekyll, in partnership with Lawrence Weaver, wrote about sixty years ago as *Gardens for Small Country Houses*, it is possible to follow the mainstream of development since 1945.

Truism though it is, gardens reflect the people who create them and the eras in which they are created. The patrician Whig élite who transformed our countryside in the eighteenth century with their sweeping landscapes were very different from the Victorian industrialists of a century later who revelled in displays of lobelia, geranium and heliotrope. And yet, varied though they have been, British gardens have never appeared in historical isolation. Rather they have been—and are—products of a selection process between acceptance and dismissal of what has gone before, and of the different factors at play at the time of their creation.

In many ways the post-Second World War period is far more complex than its predecessors. While British gardens have never been more fêted and celebrated, historic gardens are under continual threat. At the same time popular interest in gardens and gardening has exploded, with varied consequences, good and bad. Obsessed as we have become with the preservation of our past and even though strenuous efforts are made to protect and preserve, circumstances now make this difficult. And while the quantity and diversity of gardens may be growing, the creation of great gardens becomes increasingly rare.

It may of course be premature to survey a period when most of the people involved are still active and some of their gardens have yet to reach maturity. Should they not be made to stand the test of time? Should we wait to see what influence and importance—if any—they have historically? However, I would reply that nowhere is the test of time more fickle than in the survival of gardens from one generation to the next. A house, once built, is complete. It is also inorganic. A garden is alive and, whatever the aspiration of its creator, its survival is often more a case of luck than judgement.

Since the Second World War the secure continuity of gardens has been made difficult by the fact that, in an overwhelming number of cases, they have become increasingly personal. This aspect will be discussed in detail, but the point is worth making that, where possible, I have talked about the gardens with their creators in order to find out what they have been trying to achieve and why they have planned and planted their gardens in the way they have done. If the insights I have gained have made me less dismissive or critical, I feel sure that this is both right and proper.

Any talk of the threats to today's gardens should not, however, give the impression of a gloomy overall picture. Gardens have always been under threat from the next generation, as was shown conclusively during the first half of the eighteenth century when the idea of a garden as a natural landscape rapidly began to engulf the more formal style of sixteenth- and seventeenth-century traditions. On the contrary, the developing picture of gardens during the post-Second World War period is full of excitement, energy and achievement. There may be trends and characteristics which purists deplore and condemn; but ranged against such criticisms are gardens which have been created despite post-war gloom and an economic climate which has been unfavourable. These, together with the increasing number of dedicated gardeners, prove that our centuries-old tradition is as tenacious as ever.

It was this, more than anything else which encouraged me to write this book. Even if it is not immediately apparent what direction that tradition is now following, that is no cause for dismay. It did not usually bother our gardening ancestors. Whether any gardens I describe will prove, by surviving into the future, to have intrinsic and lasting qualities is a subject on which at present one can only speculate. The great thing is that the tradition was revived after six years of enforced stagnation and destruction such as had never before afflicted

British gardens. Although I do not pretend that this book provides the answer, a comment by Arthur Hellyer, which appeared in *Country Life* in 1987 is particularly relevant.

> Maybe one day a historian will explain why there was such a marvellous burst of garden-making during the two decades that followed the Second World War. At the end of that terrible conflict I remember thinking with sadness that all the great gardens of Britain had now been bankrupted by the war and crippling taxation would prevent the accumulation of new wealth to finance the creation of new gardens.
>
> In fact the reverse has happened and many gardens made, great and small, picturesque and formal. Seldom has there been such a proliferation of inventiveness, such deep understanding of plants, so much concern for the most effective combinations of colour and form. Nor, I think, had there previously been such widespread conviction that garden-making is within the competence of ordinary people with minimum help from professionals. This self-confidence also added to the diversity of the gardens created.

I would only add that I hope that the subsequent chapters show how the 'burst of garden-making' has not been just limited to the first two decades after the war, but continued since.

Given the fact that newly created gardens over forty acres are a rare species, as indeed they have been for most of this century, one of my most surprising discoveries is the number of substantial gardens that since the war have been created in private ownership. It is this category of garden which will be described in the various chapters that follow and of which details are given in the Gazetteer.

Gardens are not as easy to pigeon-hole as are houses. For instance, it would not have been possible for me to divide the chapters of my book and the gardens described, by professional designers, as the chapters of *The Latest Country Houses* are divided by architect. The reason is that, with the majority of the gardens, no professional at all was involved. This is not to say that professional designers and plantsmen have not played an important role. Their work in specific gardens and their often considerable influence through books is frequently mentioned throughout and is discussed in detail in chapter 3. If the number of people who can afford to employ them is limited, this was certainly also the case before the war. What is different now is that the urge to create one's own garden has grown much stronger.

I have decided to group the gardens into chapters on a loose basis of style. To a certain extent any such divisions are arbitrary, so I have attempted to link the chapters by discussing points of more general interest and relevance. Above all, it is the relationship between the individual characteristics and qualities of the gardens, and the general surroundings and context within which they have been created that always strikes me as of paramount importance.

Compared to the builders of post-war country houses the garden-makers are a more varied group. Country houses have been built as focal points for substantial estates, as has been the case for centuries. They have also been built largely by people whose families did the same thing in the past and, as often as not, a new house has replaced great-grandfather's or grandfather's which proved to be too large, a financial drain and impossible to run without staff. As a result the great majority of builders share a number of readily discernible points in common, not least their social origins and the strong territorial instinct of which building a country house can be seen as the crowning achievement.

No such recognizable common ground exists among their gardening counterparts. In some cases, admittedly, the backing of a farming enterprise or estate has played an important part. At the other end of the scale, however, many of the gardens cover the full extent of their owner's property. Certainly such people do not originate from the same social background as each other and this, even though it may make generalization difficult, is undoubtedly refreshing.

Linking the two groups of house-builders and garden-makers is a select band of people who have done both. Their gardens do not always rank as outstanding but they are of particular interest in that they demonstrate how a large house and garden have been planned together. In most cases the architect of the house has had something to say in the planning of the surrounding garden—even if only the 'hard' features (walls, paths, steps, gateways, etc.)—and in virtually no instance has a country house been built without some plan for the garden being drawn up immediately.

I should now perhaps describe how the gardens which feature in this book have been 'collected'. They all come under the broad umbrella of being fairly substantial country gardens. In some ways, inevitably perhaps, the choice has been both arbitrary and personal. I have, however, attempted to include those gardens which have come already to be generally recognized as 'important' or of special quality. I have also aimed to embrace the considerable variety which exists in the hope of covering the whole spectrum. They are nearly all privately owned, the exceptions being some National Trust properties, although even here most of the gardens were made by private individuals and handed on to the Trust subsequently.

Also, the majority of the gardens is in England and Wales, mainly because most Scottish and Irish gardens are part of different and quite individual traditions. If there are omissions, and I fear there are, the reason is probably to be found in gardeners being often modest people who disguise their horticultural lights. Unfortunately, while no great house can be built without written plans, a garden can be made and yet leave no record of its creation.

Coniston Cold. The portico of the old house retained as a feature of the new garden.

Coniston Cold, a new house and a new garden. Looking towards the house across the slope cleared of trees to allow the view down to the lake. The planting round the house was designed by Lanning Roper.

Detailed knowledge then can only be gained by word of mouth, which often does not spread widely or quickly.

Can one discern a predominant style in the gardens of the period which are discussed in this book? The short answer is 'no', but most important, perhaps, is the fact that, although a surprising number of gardens may have drawn ideas or inspiration from the same limited number of sources, the end-products have never been the same because of varying terrain and climate and because a free rein has been given to individual interpretation. It is precisely this individuality that is one of the most exciting characteristics of post-war gardens. Nevertheless, while there may be no one dominant style there are certain features which have assumed widespread importance. These involve the gardens' original conception, their design, planting and later maintenance, and point to what have been recurring factors that influence garden-makers as well as what has at one time or another been fashionable.

There is one fundamental characteristic of garden making evident since 1945 which represents a radical departure from the past, and to an extent it is a result of the war. Our predecessors, especially those who made gardens on a large scale, did so mostly from positions of stability and security. Their gardens were conscious statements and, if they were not as decisive as the building of a house, they were definitely confident. In recent years the creation of a garden has been inspired from the opposite end of the spectrum—as part of a search for that same stability and security. At a time when the natural world surrounding us, be it in the form of wild orchids in English hedgerows or tropical rain forests, is increasingly threatened, a garden has come to be seen as the domestic manifestation of that natural world and, as such, something to be sought after, treasured and recognized as our own ecological response to that threat. A garden has thus become a retreat from the often confusing and ugly world we live in. At no time was this more apparent than during the years immediately after the Second World War when the country stood between six years of destruction and an uncertain future.

PART I
THE BACKGROUND

1
GARDENS IN POST-WAR BRITAIN

The immediate effect of the Second World War upon British gardens was catastrophic. Gardens all over the country, large and small, were either abandoned, requisitioned or turned over to food production as part of the 'Dig for Victory' campaign. Even the formal parterre below the windows of the private royal apartments at Windsor Castle was filled with cabbages, albeit planted with decorative regularity. The situation was eloquently described by Miles Hadfield in *Gardening in Britain* (1960): 'But as the long fine autumn drew near, war broke out. Gardens were turned to the production of food, lawns were ploughed, armed forces and ammunition dumps filled our great mansions and "Capability" Brown landscapes. The pleasures of the art of gardening retreated into their remotest elysium, to be a dream that might come true with the return of peace.'[1]

Large country gardens suffered in the same way as the houses they surrounded. For most of the upper classes the inter-war years had brought no dramatic change in their way of life and at the outbreak of war in 1939 their gardens and, to a lesser extent, their houses, were both still labour-intensive. Mechanization was in its infancy and gardeners were generally employed at a ratio of one man per acre. In larger establishments, which maintained hothouses and extensive kitchen gardens, there were more. In a matter of months most of this vital labour force was removed as men volunteered or were called up. Hard on their departure came—almost inevitably—requisition. The majority of English country houses were occupied during the war, if not for military use then as schools or hospitals or to house evacuees from the cities. For those that did become hosts to the military their parks and gardens often disappeared under Nissen huts, while lawns and flower-beds were ploughed up.

Even those places which escaped being taken over ceased ornamental gardening. Everyday rudimentary maintenance usually proved impossible and without this, let alone regeneration, gardens slipped into decay. In the circumstances it was surprising—almost miraculous—that there were any survivors, usually in chancy or unusual circumstances. John Vass, head gardener at Sissinghurst in Kent, seems to have got his priorities right with his parting remark before joining the RAF in 1941: 'Look after the hedges. We can get the rest back later.'[2] At Sissinghurst his request was heeded and the same happened at other places, although not always so easily. At Packwood House in Warwickshire the huge yew trees of the celebrated 'Sermon on the Mount' garden were kept clipped by Packwood's owner, Mr Baron Ash, with the help of the inmates of a nearby juvenile lunatic asylum. At Haseley Court in Oxfordshire the equally famous topiary chess garden (planted in 1850, around the same time as Packwood's 'Sermon on the Mount') was kept in shape by one old man from the village of Little Haseley who, solely on his own initiative, came up every year to clip the intricate yew figures. Yet even if maintenance was possible it was not always popular. When Lord Fairhaven continued to add to his already extensive new garden at Anglesey Abbey in Cambridgeshire, begun in 1930, some people murmured their disapproval.

The great parks did not normally suffer in quite as drastic a way as gardens unless they were damaged—wilfully or accidentally—by military marauders. At the end of the war it was relatively easy to return large fields of parkland to their usual state of permanent grassland. In fact the interlude of cultivated crops did most of them a great deal of good. Their trees—the vital features—were usually safe as the war did not bring an excessive demand for timber. More likely to be damaged were temples or follies or other ornamental buildings. Servicemen of all nationalities seem to have had an insatiable urge to be remembered by carving their initials on pillars, steps or walls.

Country-house gardens before the war, with a few notable exceptions, were conventional and, in many cases, dull. They were ornamental and important principally for the role they played in the country-house way of life that emerged as the Victorians turned from making money to enjoying it and that managed to survive the 1914–18 war, if in somewhat reduced circumstances. There were usually some special architectural features: sunken gardens with terraces or retaining walls, gateways, small buildings or pergolas, not only because building materials and labour were cheap, but also because of the widespread influence and popularity of the style evolved by the partnership of Gertrude Jekyll and Sir Edwin Lutyens. In attempts to emulate the planting skills of Gertrude Jekyll herbaceous borders became almost obligatory, as were formal rose gardens filled with neat beds of hybrid tea varieties. Contrary to the belief that William Robinson, the militant advocate of a natural style of gardening, had single-handed dealt a fatal blow to Victorian carpet-bedding during the twilight years of the nineteenth century, it survived with vigour into the twentieth, the greenhouses of many gardens monotonously continuing to turn out hundreds of plants to provide a display of spring annuals followed by one of gaudy summer plants.

If anything new was being introduced into gardens in the inter-war years it was perhaps more recreation than before. Wide lawns, shaded in places by ancient cedars, were battlegrounds for croquet which at this time reached the height of its popularity. Alternatively there was tennis, on the grass courts

Part of the park at Holkham, Norfolk, going under the plough in 1940.

A sunken rose garden, typical of pre-war design, with formal beds of hybrid tea varieties, urns, statues and clipped yew hedges.

whose quality was being steadily improved by advances in grass seeds, weedkillers and lawn mowers. More of a novelty were swimming pools, which, if not as widespread as they became after 1945, were certainly more ornate. In only a few cases did owners themselves do any gardening more active than 'pottering'. Gardens were looked after by gardeners, who often hardly needed to be given orders, but ran their domains smoothly from one year to the next. It was the drastic decline in their numbers after 1945 which became of fundamental importance in shaping the progress of gardens thereafter.

The physical decline of gardens during the war was both visible and tangible. At the same time changes were taking place, the outcome of which were to have a more profound effect on the post-war character of gardens than most other factors and which stemmed from social and economic factors that were affecting much of English life. Some people realized that the Second World War would bring fundamental changes in a way that did not occur after 1918. Not everyone was as gloomy as Harold Nicolson, whose wartime diaries are dotted with pessimistic asides such as, 'We shall have to walk and live Woolworth life hereafter.'[3] His garden at Sissinghurst was not only one of the rare gardens of

A curvilinear peach-house at Brechin Castle, Scotland, an example of the extensive hothouses that were still maintained between the wars.

real interest and originality, but also one which survived because he and Vita Sackville-West were among the minority of owners who gardened themselves. To most of their contemporaries, however, that was just another sign of their eccentricity—or at least Vita's.

Even if owners of country houses were not always as gloomy as Harold Nicolson they felt that the war would inevitably release forces which had been lurking not far beneath the surface during the unsettled inter-war years. Looked at from the opposite social viewpoint, these changes had not so much been lurking as kept at bay and their appearance was to be celebrated. Britain had overreached herself in maintaining her war effort, and the full extent of the deprivations and hardship imposed in pursuit of victory only became fully apparent after 1945. Although victorious she was also exhausted, nearly bankrupt, and socially and economically a fundamentally different nation from the one she had been in 1939. The depression of the 1930s had shown that economically the old world was dying but now, after the uncompromising demands of the war, governments were expected to keep their side of the bargain. The first sign of this was the landslide victory of the Labour Party in the general election of 1945. Winston Churchill might have led the nation to victory but he was not to be the man to oversee the rebuilding of Britain. It is within this broad political context that it is necessary to discuss the fate of gardens, for much of what happened to gardens was directly influenced by what happened to country houses and by the changes that were brought about in the country-house way of life.

Individually the majority of country houses emerged from the Second World War in a sorry state, so much so that, to many people, a country house and all it had traditionally involved seemed doomed to become increasingly expensive and demanding. The ownership of land, and a house whose existence was rooted in that land, had lost not only its power, but also, it seemed now, its feasibility. Events subsequently proved that this was not always the case, and in *The Latest Country Houses* John Martin Robinson discusses the success stories. All the same, there was for some time a widespread feeling that country houses, if not obsolete, were direly threatened—as the prices of the scores on the market in the 1950s showed only too clearly. If they were to survive they would have to move pretty sharply with the times.

Some owners of long-established country houses and estates adapted and carried on—as they had indeed done on many occasions in the past. Others tried and failed, or simply gave up. The restoration of their houses and gardens was often hamstrung by the building regulations brought in during the war and strictly enforced until they were abolished by the Conservative Government in 1951. These had imposed licences and rationed building materials. Geoffrey Jellicoe, whose most extensive pre-war commission had been the creation of ambitious formal gardens for Ronald and Nancy Tree around Ditchley Park in

Oxfordshire, the great Palladian mansion built by James Gibbs between 1720 and 1725, maintains that Ronald Tree finally decided to leave Ditchley after the war when he was unable to obtain the necessary licence for the small quantity of materials required for the foundations and piers for a pair of wrought-iron gates he had bought for the entrance forecourt of the house.

For those who had had enough, the decision to sell up was not always that easy to put into practice. Immediately after the war few people had either the money or the inclination to buy a large country property. Therefore it is hardly surprising that to some jittery eyes the National Trust appeared as a fairy godmother to the beleaguered landowning classes.

Although established in 1895, it was not until the 1930s that the Trust began to consider seriously the possibility of taking on responsibility for country houses and their estates. During the war years so many suddenly became threatened, however, that acquisitions began to gather pace, and continued to do so into the 1950s. The possible plight of England's architectural jewels and their supporting estates was by no one more clearly recognized than the Marquess of Lothian. The marquess died in 1942, while serving as Britain's ambassador to Washington, and it was his gift to the National Trust of Blickling Hall, his Jacobean home in Norfolk and its surrounding estate of 4,500 acres, which presented them with their first house of national importance.

Blickling Hall. The main garden front.

As the Trust's readiness to acquire properties gathered pace so did the, at times, almost unseemly scramble by owners to unburden their homes on to the Trust while, at the same time, securing hereditary life tenancies for themselves and their families. James Lees-Milne, the architectural historian who over many years used to visit prospective properties on behalf of the Trust, recalls many such incidents in his diaries. Sir Henry Fairfax-Lucy, owner of Charlecote Park in Warwickshire, told Lees-Milne curtly when he asked to see inside the house after a brief inspection of the gardens: 'There is absolutely no need. Charlecote is known to be one of the great, *the* greatest houses in England.'[4]

The National Trust's policy of acquisition took a decisive step forward when they took on their first garden purely on its own merits. In 1948 it was given Hidcote Manor by the garden's creator, Major Lawrence Johnston. The recognition that gardens, as well as houses, were of national importance marked a new departure. It played a decisive role in shaping people's growing awareness of the British gardening heritage—a word that was hardly used in this context before the war—and, as a result, their interest in gardens and gardening as a whole.

The austerities of the post-war years, following hard on the heels of the hardships of wartime, turned many people's minds to the simpler pleasures of life. Nature began to be appreciated whereas before the war it had usually been taken for granted. Many people found that the easiest and most rewarding way to get close to nature was in a garden. For some, growing vegetables during the war had been their first taste of gardening. Not only had they enjoyed it, but the step from potatoes to roses was not a difficult one. Others were spurred on by the depressed state of gardens all around them. At the same time gardens took on a significance beyond the purely practical. They played an almost symbolic role in the creation of a new and better Britain. In 1947 a new hybrid tea rose called 'Peace' was introduced. It was hugely popular for many years afterwards, not only because of its toughness, resistance to disease and abundant, showy flowers, but also because of the happy overtones of its name. In *The History of the Rose* Allen Paterson gives 'Peace' pride of place among all modern roses and writes of it 'bursting upon a war-weary world'. He goes on to describe its colour as, 'a pale yellow, with pink tints towards the edge of the petals and, as the open flower ages, this pink is gradually suffused through the yellow, like the light of dawn replacing the moon'.

In 1908 the essayist E. V. Lucas wrote, 'Naomi tells me that gardening has become as fashionable as motoring.'[5] If he had been alive in the 1950s he would have said the same, but now there was an important connection between the two. By the late 1950s comparative prosperity had begun to replace austerity. The rapid growth in the number of families with motor cars and the general advent of the weekend brought about by the five-day week, gave people both the leisure and freedom to travel—privileges only enjoyed by a minority before the war. One area which received a dramatic boost was garden visiting, and this in turn fuelled the ever-growing popular interest in gardens. People began to visit gardens not just for a day out but to find new ideas to take home. Also, as the demand grew in numbers of visitors, so did the supply of gardens open to the public.

In 1927 the National Gardens Scheme had first organized the opening of gardens to the public, as part of a national memorial to Queen Alexandra. There were 600 gardens open in this first year and the proceeds went—as they still do—to help retired or needy district nurses. After the war the National Gardens Scheme continued to run the majority of gardens open to the public and their figures of gardens open and the total number of visitors clearly show the ever-burgeoning interest. In 1950 a total of just over 1,000 gardens opened, were visited by just over 300,000 and brought in receipts of just over £15,000. By 1986 the figures had risen dramatically: the number of gardens open had doubled to just over 2,000, the number of visitors had reached 800,000 and the total receipts were £460,000.

Vita Sackville-West, despite her at times obsessive shyness, played as decisive a part in the popularization of gardens as anyone. She affectionately described the visitors to Sissinghurst as the 'shillingses', the entrance fee when the Sissinghurst garden was first opened in 1938. As she makes clear, first in a letter to her husband and second in an article, she enjoyed them: 'Quite a lot of people have been to see the garden, which always pleases me. How much I prefer strangers to my friends.'[6] She also explained:

> These mild, gentle men and women who invade one's garden after putting their silver token into the bowl, these true peacemakers, these inoffensive lovers of nature, in her gayest forms, these homely souls who will travel fifty miles by bus with a fox-terrier on a lead, who will pore over a label, taking notes in a penny notebook—these are some of the people I most gladly welcome and salute. Between them and myself a particular form of courtesy survives, a gardener's courtesy, in a world where courtesy is giving place to rougher things.[7]

Vita Sackville-West's importance did not only arise from her garden at Sissinghurst. In 1946 she began writing occasional gardening articles for the *Observer* which, in 1950, became the regular weekly column 'In Your Garden' that she wrote for the next eleven years until only a few months before her death in 1962. Her column was arguably the most influential piece of gardening journalism since the war but, equally important, she was one of a number of writers who began appealing to a wide and popular audience. Others were Edward Hyams, Margery Fish and Christopher Lloyd, while magazines such as *Popular Gardening* and *Amateur Gardening* began to show an equally widespread appeal and increased readership.

Sissinghurst, the garden which has been an inspiration to a generation of gardeners.

This popularization of gardens and gardening provided the background to the preservation and restoration of substantial gardens, and impetus to the creation of the new ones with which this book is concerned. For a start, it shaped the most basic difference between large post-war gardens and their predecessors—the fact that they were no longer dependent on a large staff. Before the war it would have been most unlikely for a guest arriving to stay at a country house to be greeted by his host in old corduroys, gumboots and stout leather gloves, clutching a pair of secateurs, or, equally, by the sight of his hostess's rear view protruding from a nearby border. By the 1960s it was quite normal. Of course, this is not to say that gardeners disappeared completely. Many of the people who wanted a good garden did not have the time to do all the necessary work themselves, probably only a few hours at weekends. Even so, as the numbers of gardeners was reduced so their deployment was rationalized. In real economic terms, the average gardener's wage increased from around £2 per week in 1939 to between £3 and £4 in 1945. By 1960 it was between £5 and £6 and thereafter it rose dramatically so that by 1986 it was usually something in excess of the minimum agricultural wage of nearly £100.

People might have been prepared to find the necessary money to meet these rising costs, and able to find the gardeners to do the work, if conditions had remained as they were in 1939. But they did not. The Second World War and its social aftermath ensured that there were markedly different attitudes from both ends of the spectrum. People who had gone into private service before the war because of the security it offered now felt that this was provided by the Welfare State. In an increasingly class-conscious and socially self-conscious age, to work for someone else—be it as their cook, butler, gardener or chauffeur—was no longer an accepted way of life.

If cheap labour or, at least, cheap skilled labour was something that was no longer available and of which the cost rose astronomically, a graph showing the cost of materials needed for any 'hard' or architectural features looks the same. Although he was probably not strictly accurate, it is worth remembering that the great analyser of eighteenth-century English life, Dr Johnson, propounded in 1783: 'We compute, in England, a park wall at one thousand pounds per mile.'[8] One and a half centuries later, in 1945, the cost had not risen too dramatically—to something over four thousand. By 1952, however, it had leapt to ten thousand and by 1983 anyone extravagant enough to embark on enclosing their park with bricks and mortar would be spending a staggering £160,000 per mile. These figures are based on a wall six feet high and are more relevant for a garden when looked at on the basis of the cost per yard: just over ten shillings in 1783, two pounds ten shillings in 1940, nearly six pounds in 1952 and £91.50 in 1983.[9]

These economic limitations have had an understandable influence on the appearance of gardens. 'Labour-saving', a virtually unheard-of phrase before the war, began to assume great prominence in gardening parlance—both in reference to plants and 'devices', in particular machinery. There is no doubt that revolutionary improvements in garden machinery, its wider availability and the fact that more people have had the money to buy it, have been decisive in softening the blow of reductions in garden staff. Mechanization may not have affected directly what people grow in their gardens—although technological advances have transformed propagation—but garden maintenance has been assisted decisively by self-propelled lawn mowers and rotovators, ride-on garden tractors, mechanical hedge-clippers and the many other tools and gadgets we now take for granted.

If we take them for granted today the machines were novelties to most people for many years after the war. The reaction of Rupert Hart-Davis and his wife to the arrival of their first motor-mower in 1957, which Hart-Davis describes to his correspondent for many years George Lyttelton, was typical of their contemporaries. 'Yesterday, in lovely hot sunshine, Comfort and I had our first trial of strength with the new motor-mower. Neither of us had ever operated one before, but we found it most satisfying and enjoyable, though we did more than we realized and are stiff and blistered today.' In Hart-Davis's next weekly letter to Lyttelton the mower is still worthy of mention. 'My daughter has been home for the week-end, and luckily she is fascinated by the new motor-mower.'[10]

Machines may have been a godsend but they have assisted rather than accounted for the surprising success with which owners have re-created or created and thereafter maintained large gardens since the war. At the heart of their success has been a shift in attitude. Among other things this has led to a feeling that gardens could no longer be enjoyed in a purely proprietorial manner and that some sort of active involvement is both necessary and desirable. Once they had made the step forward from managing to maintaining their gardens, the character and appearance of these gardens would be much more dictated by their own taste, likes and dislikes.

This increasing personalization of gardens combined with the almost universal minimizing of labour to bring about a dramatic reduction in the size of fruit and vegetable gardens. Before the war extensive walled kitchen gardens with rows of soft fruit and vegetables, fruit trees trained against the surrounding walls and heated greenhouses for grapes, peaches and other tender fruits, as well as plants to decorate the house, were still commonplace. Usually separated from other areas, these kitchen gardens often provided enough work to keep half the members of a garden staff of, say, six men busy throughout the year. There were many head gardeners for whom their Muscat grapes or early nectarines were their annual pride and joy, rather than any rare shrub or flower border in full bloom.

These gardens—except in the grandest establishments—have virtually disappeared since 1945. This is not to say that people have stopped growing fruit and vegetables, although, of course, their increasing availability in shops, particularly since the rise of the supermarket, has had an important effect. Instead they have rationalized their kitchen gardens, both in size and in what they grow, some people not bothering with staples such as potatoes, lettuces or apples because they are cheap and easy to buy. Instead they concentrate on a selection of favourites: asparagus, French beans or beetroot for instance.

At the same time fruit and vegetables have played a more integral part in gardens. Although the reality of the traditional cottage garden is elusive, the cottage garden ideal has strongly influenced many gardens since the war, despite the fact that the majority of them are far larger than any humble original. The ideal is a picture of flowers, fruit and vegetables growing happily and informally together. While the cottage garden has been one source of inspiration which gives fruit and vegetables an important role the French 'potager' has become another. Although nobody in England has attempted anything on the scale of the huge potager at the Loire château of Villandry, growing vegetables, fruit and herbs in a formal and decorative manner has become increasingly fashionable.

Some owners of long-established country houses, especially those brought up in the different climates of the inter-war years, let alone the Edwardian era, may have found the prospect of weeding the borders or mowing the lawn daunting if not terrifying. On the whole, however, such people took to it with alacrity and in many cases a consuming enthusiasm that, as much as anything else, has facilitated the healthy progress of their gardens.

The enthusiasm has been partly inspired by an increasingly romantic view of the countryside. If the traditional country house, with all the responsibilities of its property and its stereotyped way of life, has declined and only been continued by those whose families have lived in such a manner for generations, a house in the country—with all the pleasures and less of the responsibilities—has become an ideal widely desired. The garden has become an integral part of that ideal—a part which recalls Ford Madox Ford's picture of his perfect garden as a sanctuary, in that it answers an instinctive desire for seclusion, intimacy and security. Surrounded by the threats, uncertainty and boorishness of much of our consumer world, people have turned to gardens for solace, for the reassurance of nature and of its stability. In recent years growing public awareness of ecology and conservation—words unheard except in scientific circles before the war—has only served to intensify this desire. And if a place in the country has become increasingly desirable, for many people it has also become increasingly possible, partly as a result of more widespread prosperity and because modern transport has made it feasible to live in the country and still work in the towns and cities.

From the viewpoint of, say, 1945, those large country gardens which have been created since the war would appear to have succeeded against the odds. However, closer inspection shows that, given many of the circumstances and characteristics of the post-war decades, there has hardly been a more fertile period in our history for gardens. If the grandeur of the past is not so evident—although, as will be described in subsequent chapters, there are still loud clarion calls for horticulture and landscape design—then that is hardly surprising since it has receded from all aspects of our lives. Given the adaptability with which gardens, aided by the advent of machinery, have made the transformation from being labour-intensive, as well as their importance as a means of escape and relaxation and their significance as a central part of the threatened natural world, it is not surprising that many people have seen the creation of a garden as one of their life's ambitions. They are surely right in this; and if their gardens have faults, they are characteristic faults of our society in general—a desire to have everything yesterday and an unwillingness to plan for the future.

2
FOUNDATIONS OF A TRADITION

Since the Second World War garden-makers have borrowed more freely from the past than ever before. They have also borrowed more widely, and the post-war garden is perhaps best described as a glorious mongrel. This is in no way derogatory; rather it conjures up a picture of healthy vitality and of the almost limitless possibilities for character and appearance which derive from a varied ancestry. Certainly it is impossible to generalize about country gardens in the same way as one can about post-war country houses, the majority of which are hybrids from a Georgian specie.

Of course, this variety and versatility is not purely stylistic. The post-war garden has often had to be a creature with many different purposes: a place not only for growing plants but also for allowing children and pets the space and trappings they need: swings, slides, sand-pits and pens. This is in part an outdoor extension of the house itself, providing a place for enjoying barbecues which has a reassuring unity with the house, as well as offering recreation with, perhaps, a swimming pool and a tennis court discreetly incorporated.

Not everyone was happy, however, about the way so many British gardens looked to the past for their inspiration. In 1938, just before the Second World War, the landscape architect Christopher Tunnard wrote:

> Contemporary garden design has not even yet caught up with contemporary trends in architecture. It is to be hoped that in the near future garden makers will become aware of this fact, and that instead of re-hashing old styles to fit new buildings they will create something more expressive of the contemporary spirit and something more worthy of the tradition to which they are the heirs.[1]

Tunnard was hoping that modernism would spread from architecture to gardening—which it did not, and, partly through disenchantment and a feeling that Americans were more receptive, he emigrated to the United States in 1939. By the end of the war it was even less likely to do so and the post-war decades have seen a surging interest in our gardening past and an acceptance that our outstanding gardens are not only worth preserving but also worthy models. Modern gardens, in the sense that Tunnard was hoping for, have been created, but very rarely in the country and they have been individual, not part

A Barbara Hepworth abstract sculpture in a garden setting—the sort of modern feature that Christopher Tunnard advocated.

of a widespread trend. Most owners have wanted their gardens to be natural, traditional and soothing; not places for the restless innovation, controversy or unease which are so often the hallmarks of modernism.

Although the Second World War marked a downturn in the fortunes of British gardens its outcome meant that most people—either by choice or force of circumstance—were able to plan gardens from a fresh starting-point. They did so with a keen awareness of the past which was highlighted by Geoffrey Jellicoe who, unlike Tunnard, has become a central figure in British garden design. 'The resolution of the ethos of past history with that of present owner is perhaps the most interesting and compelling challenge in garden design.'[2] The challenge is the same whether, as in Jellicoe's case, you are a professional designing for others, or whether you are planning your own humble plot.

More democratic and domestic attitudes and reductions in staff have meant many more people actively planning and, to some degree, maintaining their own gardens. As their involvement has become more personal so has their whole approach, producing an overwhelming tendency to pick and choose liberally from the Aladdin's Cave of available styles and plants, and work them together into a garden whose origins may be numerous but whose guiding hand is its owner's. It is quite possible for a garden made since the war to contain a knot garden from the sixteenth century, a formal *allée* leading to a statue or urn from the seventeenth, perhaps a sweep of grass leading down to a lake from the eighteenth, an arboretum from the nineteenth, and an herbaceous border or series of small enclosures from the twentieth century.

While this has potentially suggested gardens of limitless variety, it has also caused considerable problems. Faced with such a bewildering variety of styles and such a vast quantity of plants available, the effect on many people and their gardens has been confusion. The tendency towards too much of everything has led away from the most basic principle not only of design but also of planting: restraint. In *Garden Design* Sylvia Crowe pin-points the effects they can have: 'The lack of peace in the English gardens of to-day is intensified because, although throughout history garden traditions have fertilized each other, never before have there been so many cross-currents and so little opportunity for the flood of ideas to evolve a tradition adapted to local currents.' She adds: 'The diversity of plant material now available to us is often blamed for the lack of design in the majority of English gardens. But the real fault lies in lack of discrimination and restraint.'[3]

This catholic approach to planning and planting a garden is not surprising, since British gardens ceased to follow one main tradition over a hundred years ago and turned towards increasing diversity. The seeds were sown at the end of the era of the eighteenth-century landscape when, with the rise of a wealthy middle class, gardening was no longer the exclusive domain of the landowning oligarchy who had previously been running—as well as owning—the country. At this time John Claudius Loudon (1783–1843) emerged as a figure of increasing importance through his writing on gardening. Born the son of a humble Scottish farmer and dogged throughout his life by ill-health and financial disaster, through the books and magazines he produced during the last twenty years of his life Loudon can claim to be the founder of modern gardening. It is a melancholy thought that it was the spectre of his creditors that accounted for the staggering output of words that he achieved with the help of his devoted wife Jane, herself a novelist, botanist and early protagonist in the struggle for freedom for women.

Loudon's major achievements were an *Encyclopaedia of Gardening*, first published in 1822, *The Gardener's Magazine* established in 1826 and the eight volumes of the definitive *Arboretum et Fruiticetum Britannicum* (*The Trees and Shrubs of Great Britain, Native and Foreign*) published in 1838. While the encyclopaedia was the first such book to treat the subject of gardening from every angle *The Gardener's Magazine* was the first popular gardening magazine. Both enjoyed a wide readership and influence. Most revealing of his understanding of the direction gardening was taking was the publication of *The*

Sissinghurst. One of the garden's many views to the various buildings,
here looking from the Moat Walk to the South Cottage and the Tower.

Sissinghurst. The Nuttery.

'Peace': a symbol of the revival of Britain's gardening
tradition after the Second World War.

Detail of a decorative 'potager'.

Suburban Gardener and Villa Companion in 1838 in which Loudon welcomed the Victorian middle class to the delights of gardening. He managed to reconcile the differences of the natural style of the eighteenth-century landscapes and the formality of previous periods. The result was the 'gardenesque' style that he evolved, that provided foundations on which gardeners have built ever since.

> By the gardenesque style is to be understood the production of that kind of scenery which is best calculated to display the individual beauty of trees, shrubs and plants in a state of nature; the smoothness and greenness of lawns; and the smooth surfaces, curved directions, dryness and firmness of gravel walks; in short, it is calculated for displaying the art of the gardener.[4]

Not all gardeners today are students of garden history or acquainted at first hand with Loudon's writing, but there are few for whom his words are not relevant.

Despite his influence, Loudon cannot be blamed for the extremes of Victorian gardening: huge conservatories, hothouses and winter gardens heated by boilers big enough to drive steam engines, or vast parterres filled with vibrant annuals, which were produced in their thousands in ranges of greenhouses. His reaction would have been disapproving, but no doubt more temperate than that of the irascible William Robinson (1838–1935) who, driven almost to a state of frenzied anger by the excesses of high-Victorianism, in 1883 published *The English Flower Garden*. He had already, in 1870, published *The Wild Garden* and, in 1871, founded *The Garden*, a weekly magazine soon to be followed by *Gardening Illustrated*. Robinson dedicated the first issue of *The Garden* to Loudon and he is, chronologically, the next major influence on the modern garden.

Robinson came from even humbler origins than Loudon—Irish rather than Scottish—but he was to become a figure of revolutionary importance in British gardens. Virtually no evidence of his work as a gardener survives, other than perhaps a little at his own home, Gravetye Manor, but his impact was made primarily as a writer and in his fervent advocacy of a natural style of gardening. By allowing the shape of a garden to be dictated by its natural site, by growing hardy British plants—as well as ones from overseas—in an unregimented fashion, and by bringing into the garden the wild flowers which filled the English countryside, Robinson established trends that continue strongly today. In discussing *The English Garden*, where Robinson refers to 'the existing gardens' meaning those of his natural school, Miles Hadfield concludes: 'The "existing gardens" exemplify the triumph of the "natural" style of gardening evolved by Robinson and his school, which is in general the style that has been maintained—perhaps only under the force of economic circumstances—ever since.'[5]

When Robinson had earned enough money to buy a place in the country he chose the derelict house and garden site of Gravetye Manor in Sussex. He was not the first person to do this, but he publicized the possibility of 'buying-up and doing-up' which has continued ever since. His mantle was taken up very quickly, while he was still alive, by Gertrude Jekyll, to whom posterity has given a wider reputation and, perhaps, the credit for some of Robinson's innovations. Jekyll also achieved considerable acclaim as a writer, starting with articles for *The Garden*, but she was far more active and successful as a practical gardener. Paintings and photographs of Gertrude Jekyll conjure up an image of a kind of Mrs Tiggy-Winkle of gardening, a dumpy figure with grey hair tied in a bun, working in numerous gardens in the stout leather boots immortalized in the painting of them by William Nicholson.

Gertrude Jekyll was a plantswoman *par excellence*. She was also a talented artist and this played a large part in her gardening style. Following and adapting the principles laid down by Robinson, she established what have been seen since as some of the most important qualities of the 'English garden': plant associations, careful balance of colour and a highly critical approach to plants used. Although it is almost certain that none of her planting schemes survive in their original form—and few gardeners today plan a garden in the kind of minute detail that she did—Gertrude Jekyll's general principles of planting are among the main foundations of the modern British garden.

Her individual talents notwithstanding, it was in her partnership with the architect Edwin Lutyens, which began in the 1890s, that Gertrude Jekyll's work achieved its most complete success. They shared a love of vernacular architecture and the use of local building materials, and it was not difficult for Gertrude Jekyll to instil in the young architect a growing interest in garden architecture. Soon he had evolved his own firm principles of design: 'Every garden scheme should have a back-bone, a central idea beautifully phrased. Every wall, path, stone and flower should have its relationship to the central idea.'[6]

Together they achieved a fusion between formality and informality, between architecture and gardening, which has been one of the most sought-after ideals of gardeners ever since. They stressed the need for a unity between house and garden which Lutyens achieved with strict design and architectural features, and which Jekyll clothed with planting. Formality around the house should gently merge into informality in more distant areas of the garden. One can scarcely count the number of people who since the Second World War have created a garden in pursuit of this elusive goal.

In 1896 Lutyens designed a house for Gertrude Jekyll herself, at Munstead Wood near Godalming, in Surrey—the county where they were to carry out a great number of their commissions over the next thirty years. The garden contained a courtyard and terrace, nut-walk, pergola, a main flower—or herbaceous—border, a kitchen garden with flowers, fruit and vegetables, a

34

Gravetye Manor, William Robinson's home, in springtime.

hidden garden and spring garden and large areas of natural woodland, as well as doorways, walls, seats and other architectural features designed by Lutyens. For Miles Hadfield the garden is 'probably of greater significance in the history of gardening than Stowe or any other of our British precedents'.[7]

These different individuals can be seen as the major originators of the modern garden in its many different forms, but a more general development began to take place from the early decades of the nineteenth century, and continued for over a century, which has also had a dramatic impact and accounts for much of the variety in today's gardens. This concerned the swelling influx of plants coming from abroad, ranging from lofty Douglas Firs from British Columbia (named after the intrepid collector, David Douglas, who first introduced them to Britain) to rhododendrons from China and the tiniest Alpine flowers. Apart from the tender exotics from tropical climates—whose introduction was little more than horticultural gimmickry and which have always had to be confined to greenhouses or conservatories—Britain's maritime temperate conditions proved a more than suitable home for the great majority of the introductions. The characters and adventures of the men who

35

Munstead Wood, Gertrude Jekyll's home. She planned and planted the garden with Edwin Lutyens.

Munstead Wood, the summer borders.

collected these plants are many and various; Douglas himself suffered a fearful death during an expedition to Hawaii in 1834, when aged thirty-five, he fell into a pit-trap made to catch wild cattle which already contained one of these animals. Primarily botanists and horticulturalists, the men were as much a part of the growing British Empire as the missionaries in Africa and the civil servants in India. Their journeys to New Zealand, the Himalayas, the Rocky Mountains and almost every other part of the temperate world were often intrepid excursions into little-known areas and Douglas was not the only one to die in the quest for rare species.

John Loudon had argued that a garden was primarily for the display of plants, and the continuous flow into Britain of trees, shrubs and flowers from overseas ensured that the appearance of gardens would in the future have almost limitless possibilities, so wide was the range available. What people now chose to plant would be dictated, to a certain extent, by changing fashions, but more predominantly by personal taste.

Given this general background, people creating gardens since the Second World War have been strongly influenced by what they can see. Ideas and inspiration have been found more in other gardens than in books and, as a result, this has led to a number of gardens—such as Hidcote and Sissinghurst —mostly created in the twentieth century, becoming widely emulated models of almost legendary fame. These gardens may be well known, but it is important to appreciate precisely why they have attained their considerable reputations and to understand the influence, direct or indirect, which they have had on so many gardens since 1945.

It is universally acknowledged—by both professional and amateur gardeners—that, in the creation of his garden at Hidcote Manor, Major Lawrence Johnston achieved a rare masterpiece. The genius of the garden lies in its completeness and almost limitless variety. As Edward Hyams wrote, it is 'the master work of the twentieth century; and, as such, bringing together in itself an expression of all the principal styles and traditions of English garden-ing in a brilliantly successful combination.'[8]

Better than a detailed description, a brief analysis will, I hope, outline why the garden has had so much influence. For a start it is not intimidating: the house is a modest Cotswold manor and the scale of the garden is in perfect harmony with its size. Because the garden was created by one man during his lifetime the atmosphere is intimate and personal, even today nearly thirty years after Lawrence Johnston's death. Many people have been inspired and encouraged by the uncompromising character of the site with which he began, perched on a windswept Cotswold hilltop, and seeing the way in which he overcame it; for instance, making hedges, so necessary for shelter, into the garden's framework.

If the garden contains an inexhaustible supply of riches, they are presented in a wonderfully digestible manner. The series of enclosures lead one from another, each with its own character, and their secrecy and surprise is the ideal foil to the three main vistas of the Theatre Lawn, the Red Borders and Stilt Garden, and the Long Walk. Although to many people the Hidcote style is a garden of enclosures there is a great deal more, not least the planting along the stream and in the woodland garden. As far as the plants themselves are concerned, Lawrence Johnston was a plantsman, plant collector and botanist and, if much of the actual planting has been changed since 1948 when the National Trust took over the garden, the range and quality still reflect the immense and critical knowledge that went into the original choice.

Lawrence Johnston was a reticent man made famous by his garden. By contrast, the careers of Harold Nicolson and Vita Sackville-West have added to the reputation of the garden they created at Sissinghurst Castle, in Kent. The Nicolsons knew and admired Lawrence Johnston and Hidcote, whose creation was nearly complete when they bought the derelict Sissinghurst in 1930, and the two gardens are sufficiently different to show conclusively how infinitely adaptable the ideal of the modern garden had become. At the same time

Hidcote Manor. The Stilt Garden where clipped hornbeams continue the axis of the Red Borders.

Sissinghurst is in many ways in the Hidcote mould, and the appeal of the gardens has similarities. Each possesses an enviable harmony between design and planting. At Sissinghurst the design was Harold Nicolson's domain, while Vita Sackille-West carried out most of the planting. Again, the gardens offer infinite variety, and intimacy, surprise and secrecy are intrinsic features of both. In the division into enclosures and different areas, which seemed as natural at Sissinghurst as at Hidcote, the Nicolsons started with some of the divisions already provided by brick walls and the heterogeneous collection of buildings which comprise the castle.

The similarities are, however, academic. They are only important because the similar goals which Lawrence Johnston and the Nicolsons were pursuing have become the goals of their numerous admirers. They have certainly found the charm of Sissinghurst unique, fundamentally because of the small scale on which the component parts of the garden are planned. The series of enclosed rooms—a term which has been greatly over-used in descriptions of gardens, but which can be accurately applied to Sissinghurst—are of a size with which visitors to the garden have instantly been able to identify. There are no sweeping lawns or grand vistas which the visitor, perhaps looking for ideas for his or her own garden, might find impressive but too formidable. For all his insistence on firm and obvious overall design, Harold Nicolson spoke for the mass of contemporary English gardeners, at the same time as indirectly pin-pointing the qualities most of them feel that he and Vita achieved at Sissinghurst, when he wrote:

> I admit that Versailles, Courances and Villandry are superb achievements of the architectural school of gardening. Yet a garden is intended for the pleasure of its owner and not for ostentation. Nobody could sit with his family on the parterre of Versailles and read the Sunday papers while sipping China tea. Nobody who really cares for flowers can want them arranged in patterns as if they were carpets from Shiraz or Isfahan. Most civilized people prefer the shade of some dear family tree to the opulence of a parterre, displaying its pattern under the wide open sky.[9]

The intimacy of the garden's scale exaggerates the profusion of the planting and, together, these two factors lie at the heart of Sissinghurst's popularity and influence. The profusion is the creation of the female hand of Vita Sackville-West whose romantic attitude to the garden was brought to life in the plants with which she filled it: old-fashioned roses, lilacs and other traditional English plants. She wanted the garden to be, as she herself put it, 'a tumble of roses and honeysuckle, figs and vines. It was a romantic place and, within the austerity of Harold Nicolson's straight lines, must be romantically treated.'[10]

Whether it is Sissinghurst's white garden, the old-fashioned rose garden, or the lime walk with its carpet of spring bulbs on both sides of the paved path, they have all become models which many thousands of visitors have aspired to emulate. Parts of the garden—not only the area called the Cottage Garden—invoke the feeling of a traditional cottage garden developed to an idealized state. And yet this scarcely begins to cover the garden's breadth of character; its inspiration is not only English but also French and Italian, the planting, if ebullient, is too sophisticated in its variety and continuity through the year and the design too clever for such a description. The easy naturalness of the atmosphere derives from its sense of place; it is as much part of the Kentish countryside that surrounds it and as harmonious with the red brick walls of the old buildings as its two creators hoped it would be and certainly they were both acutely conscious of Jellicoe's 'ethos of past history'.

Although not truly post-Second World War in that much of the garden was laid out and planted during the 1930s, Sissinghurst was continued thereafter by the Nicolsons. It was also after the war that Vita Sackville-West began to boost the interest in her garden with her weekly column in the *Observer*. In a similar manner, another gardener who had enormous influence through her writing was Margery Fish, who began making her garden at East Lambrook Manor in Somerset in 1938 and continued there until her death in 1969. Although since then the garden has changed, during the 1960s Margery Fish's books made it a place of pilgrimage. Her first book, *We Made a Garden*, was published in 1956 and described how she and her husband created what she hoped would be a 'typical cottage garden'. East Lambrook lacked the formality and architecture of either Hidcote or Sissinghurst but this only served to heighten the effects that Margery Fish did achieve with plants. If the informal, almost random style of her plant associations was the product of great skill and knowledge, Margery Fish struck an immediate chord with people because she began gardening at East Lambrook with no previous experience. At the same time as increasing general awareness of the need to understand the individual qualities of many plants, more than anyone else Margery Fish popularized the 'cottage garden effect' as a country garden ideal.

On a far larger scale than East Lambrook, Hidcote or Sissinghurst is a garden that was created to achieve a different effect from these three and that has to an extent provided the impetus—or at least a leading example—for another style of modern garden. Westonbirt Arboretum is no more a garden for some people than a 'Capability' Brown landscape. It is a collection of trees, but, as such, it exemplifies what has become an increasing fascination for many garden-makers and demonstrates in an unrivalled manner how such a collection should be displayed. It is also arguably the most comprehensive celebration of those numerous species that, brought to Britain from abroad, have enriched our landscape.

The arboretum was begun as early as 1829 by the Holford family who carried on over three generations right into the twentieth century. Their planting shows an uncanny appreciation of the form and colour of trees, as well as of the area they need when in full maturity. The quantities of different varieties are positioned to be shown off to their best individual advantage and—most significant—Westonbirt was one of the first places to reveal on a large scale the outstanding autumn foliage of many of the imported trees which has subsequently become such a popular reason for planting them. Even Lawrence Johnston acknowledged his debt to Westonbirt by naming the area of woodland garden at Hidcote after it.

Some gardens are blessed with a site with many natural advantages. Others have few, but whichever is the case it has become increasingly recognized that to make the most of these features, and create a garden sympathetic to them, is a high priority. This recognition has been encouraged by the example of a number of existing gardens and possibly by none more than Bodnant in North Wales. The garden is on a south-west facing slope, with a mild climate and abundant water in streams, while the valley of the River Conwy and the hills of Snowdonia beyond provide a dramatic backdrop.

In addition to its site it is the combination of the formal style of gardening in the terraces descending the slope and the naturally planted areas below that are filled with flowering trees and shrubs that has given Bodnant its uniqueness as a modern garden. If few people can aspire to Bodnant's scale or setting this is unimportant for, as with other gardens, it is essentially education that they are providing, not a model for copying.

Henry Pochin who, in 1875, purchased the house positioned on top of the slope, began much of the planting at Bodnant, including many of the specimen trees, the pinetum and the often copied laburnum arch. His daughter, Laura McLaren, continued to build up the gardens but it was her son, the second Lord Aberconway, who gave them their touch of genius. He began gardening at Bodnant as a young man and continued there for over half a century until his death in 1953. He bequeathed Bodnant to the National Trust.

Lord Aberconway created the terraces below the house, each with its own individual features, and added throughout the gardens the quantities of different plants of which the most famous are the rhododendrons, azaleas and camellias. In his expansion of the gardens and, notably, in the raising of the numerous outstanding plants that additionally enhanced Bodnant's reputation, Lord Aberconway was assisted by his head gardener, Frederick Puddle, a Yorkshireman who went to Bodnant as head gardener shortly after the First World War and remained there until his death, one year before Lord Aberconway's, in 1952. Puddle became renowned throughout the gardening world for his formidable horticultural prowess. He also established a family connection with Bodnant that has continued for two generations: his son Charles succeeded him as head gardener and was in his turn succeeded by his son Martin, the present head gardener.

Bodnant. Looking across one of the five descending terraces.

Bodnant has been described as 'the last great British garden combining formality, natural planting and horticultural interest of great style and scale'.[11] More ebullient—and perhaps more relevant in stressing Bodnant's influence—is Edward Hyams's conclusion:

> The men who made this garden had absorbed the earlier traditions, the traditions of formal gardening, Italianate gardening, picture gardening, so that in the laying out of the walks and plantations, and in the use of country in such a manner as would enable them to exploit the immense wealth in plant material available to them, they had the benefit of what had almost become an instinct for right design. If a visitor, anxious to know what the 'English garden' has become at last, had time for but a single garden this is the one, out of many hundreds, I would send him to.[12]

These gardens are by no means the only ones that have been sources of inspiration and education to garden-makers since the war, but they are among the foremost and make up a privileged group in terms of their reputations and quality. Their relevance derives from the fact that the history of the modern garden has come to be dominated not by stylistic schools of thought or by men who have propounded theories and carried them out, but by individual gardens and the people who have created them. The gardens themselves have set out by their visible example the guidelines that, given the limitations within which they are working, other people have tried to follow. These can be summarized as: a balance between formality and informality—ideally achieved in the relationship of design and planting, the desire for a natural style whether in all of or part of a garden, and the thoughtful use of plants in a manner best suited to any particular site and personal taste.

3
THE ROLE OF
THE PROFESSIONAL

The tendency for gardens to become increasingly personal seems at first to point to a declining role for the professional designer. Certainly only a limited number of garden owners have had either the inclination or the money to call in a professional, let alone give him a free hand in the creation of a substantial new garden. Threatened by taxation and public antipathy, the private patron has become, since 1945, a retiring species who, by and large, prefers to keep his head below the parapet. As one beleaguered owner remarked: 'It is unwise and unpopular to behave like a patrician in a plebian age.'

In the past many people wishing for gardens on an impressive scale had little desire for personal involvement. Their gardens were planned and laid out by a professional and maintained by however many gardeners were necessary. If this attitude reached an extreme during the late Victorian and Edwardian eras it certainly continued right up until 1939.

Since 1945, owners who have called in designers have unquestionably been more involved in the plans and subsequent work than, as Geoffrey Jellicoe maintains, was ever the case before. Jellicoe even argues that the whole basis of the patron or client relationship has changed. Citing the examples of Ditchley Park and Royal Lodge, Windsor, two of his principal pre-war commissions, he says that his clients, Mr and Mrs Ronnie Tree at Ditchley and King George VI and Queen Elizabeth at Royal Lodge, were content in both cases for him to suggest and carry out a plan, in a comparable manner to how 'Capability' Brown and Humphry Repton had worked for their patrons. A great many of them had been happy for the designers to impose their formula and were content to follow fashion.[1]

This is the case no longer. More often than not an aspiring garden-maker knows what he wants. What he lacks is the knowledge, experience or technical ability to carry out his ideas. Therefore he calls in a professional in order, in a sense, to unlock his thoughts and show how they can be implemented. This often means that the professional does little more than draw up the initial plans for the garden, but making an all-important contribution because he is best able to recognize the potential of different features of a site which can be highlighted and worked around from an early stage. Once provided with guidance or an overall plan many people are content to carry out the future developments, which in most cases means planting.

Despite such changes in their relationships, professionals—be they primarily designers or plantsmen—have never been more numerous. This is largely because the post-war decades have seen a considerable widening of their field of activity. Conditions were beginning to change in the 1930s, but until then substantial country gardens were their staple diet. Today an enormous trade has emerged in the design and maintenance of small, usually urban or suburban gardens. At the same time most designers have in their time created gardens for office blocks or department stores. One of Geoffrey Jellicoe's most adventurous and modernist designs was for the roof garden of Harvey's Store, in Guildford, which he carried out in the 1950s. Some years later another distinguished professional of the post-war decades, James Russell, also worked in Guildford, designing gardens for the Wiggins Teape building—this as a result of a contract Russell had with the construction firm Arup Associates.

The most important single influence, however, on professional garden design has been the emergence and expansion of the new profession of landscape architecture. Landscape architecture, as a term, had been vaguely used since the end of the nineteenth century, but always in the context of garden design. Those private individuals, whose predecessors had regularly commissioned ambitious landscapes, began to fall under siege as early as the 1880s, with the agricultural depression and the accompanying crisis of confidence in land. By the beginning of the twentieth century they were also being faced with the tax demands of the Liberal Chancellor, David Lloyd George.

Therefore the new profession did not emerge to cater for these traditional patrons. Rather it was prompted by a realization of the coming challenge for large-scale landscape work in the public sector. Since the Second World War those landowners who do have the necessary acreage—and money—are most likely to have also an existing park to maintain. Moreover, in today's economic climate they are unlikely to have the inclination to create a large-scale landscape, despite short-term incentives such as the tax concessions currently enjoyed by woodland in comparison with agricultural land. In the 1980s, if landowners feel less threatened by the Exchequer, or by Socialist dogma, than they did during the 1960s and 1970s, they are more threatened by the prospects for British farming under EEC policy and regulations.

By contrast the damage of the war and the widespread desire to create a new Britain provided the launching-pad for landscape architecture which had still been in its infancy in 1939. In Britain the profession was officially born with the foundation of the Institute of Landscape Architects (now the Landscape Institute) in 1929—some thirty years after the equivalent foundation in the United States. Twenty years later, in 1949, the International Federation of Landscape Architects was founded in Cambridge. The first President of the

Institute of Landscape Architects was Thomas Mawson, the best established professional garden designer of the day. It was indicative of the attitude of the 'old guard' that Mawson himself felt initially that the new body would be unnecessary. For him private clients were still the bread and butter of the trade and, in the circumstances, he was confident that his own firm and that of another established professional would be able to cope with all the major commissions in the immediate future.

Events were to prove otherwise. The new work lay in the landscaping of roads and the siting of power-stations and reservoirs. With the opportunities offered by the creation of the post-war 'new towns' landscape architecture came of age. Since then it has played an integral role in the growth of Britain's infrastructure and industrial development, as well as in national parks and forestry. To some extent the incentive derived from a growing concern for the landscape and the need for commercial development to be carried out in a sympathetic manner. This concern was voiced admirably by one of the founder members of the Institute, Brenda Colvin, in her book *Land and Landscape*, first published in 1948 and now a standard work.

Sutton Place. The Paradise Garden, where arbours of roses, clematis and jasmine enclose a bubbling fountain.

The control which modern man is able to exert over his environment is so great that we easily overlook the power of the environment over man. Perhaps we just assume that any environment, modified and conditioned by human activity, must inevitably be suited to human life. We know that this is not so, really, and that man can ruin his surroundings and make them unsuitable for future generations, just as he can make war and leave unsolved political problems leading to more war; but we continue to act as if we did not know it, and we have not properly mastered the methods which the elementary knowledge should lead us to apply.[2]

It might appear that landscape architecture has charted a different and detached course from garden design. That the two are inextricably linked and will always be so is clearly pointed to by one landscape architect, Michael Lancaster:

As the house can be said to be the design parameter for architects, so is the garden for landscape architects. Although there are some, such as the Brazilian, Burle Marx, who have made their reputations on the design of gardens, few can sustain a practice by such means. But there are few who do *not* design gardens, if only for themselves. In this way they can experiment and express their own ideas, uninhibited by commercial pressures and client requirements.[3]

One important side-effect of landscape architecture in Britain has been the way in which it has provided an outlet for modernist or generally progressive aspirations in garden design. Abroad, especially in California and other parts of the United States, Brazil and Scandinavia, the design of private gardens has often been closely allied to landscape architecture in design developments with the work of men such as Roberto Burle Marx and Thomas Church. While the uniquely deep roots of British gardening and the intensification of traditional attitudes to gardens after the war were bound to lead to a quite different situation, the opening up of new working areas for professionals played an important role in shaping the character of post-war gardens.

The three most distinguished British figures in landscape architecture and garden design have been Brenda Colvin, Dame Sylvia Crowe and Sir Geoffrey Jellicoe. Dame Sylvia and Sir Geoffrey both received their honours for services to the profession while Brenda Colvin was appointed CBE. Dame Sylvia and she are best known for their many large-scale landscape projects, such as the siting of reservoirs and power-stations and a number of urban developments including, in Dame Sylvia's case, the new towns of Basildon, Harlow, Warrington and Washington.

At the same time both their careers have included designs for a number of private gardens and reveal the fundamental relationship between landscape and garden. Brenda Colvin's garden design was best displayed in her own garden at Little Peacocks, Filkins, Gloucestershire, and in her description of her aims.

> The planting is intended to give continuous calm enjoyment at all seasons, rather than dazzle the eye in the height of summer. The ground is well covered with low plants chosen for beauty of foliage: many are evergreen and there are masses of spring bulbs. In and over the ground-cover plants are many flowering shrubs, roses, viburnums, hydrangeas, tree peonies, etc., to provide flower all through the year . . . I have tried to get a feeling of quiet space in this small area, enclosed as it is by grey stone walls and farm buildings. I try, too, to engender a sense of anticipation and interest by the progression from one interesting plant group to the next in a rhythm, giving definite contrasts without loss of unity. But it is difficult to reconcile simplicity with one's enthusiasm for plants in so small a garden, and I probably let the plants jostle one another too much.[4]

It was partly thanks to help from Brenda Colvin and Geoffrey Jellicoe that Sylvia Crowe was able to establish herself in private practice after the war and for many years she and Brenda Colvin shared an office. Both of them worked on the twin beliefs that any garden—however small—is landscape in miniature and that work on any landscape should be guided by the principles of garden design as they have evolved through history. For Sylvia Crowe private gardens are 'the gloriettas of the individual man' within the surrounding landscape and her ideas were expressed in her classic book, *Garden Design*, first published in 1958.

Geoffrey Jellicoe's reputation is based on his work as a garden designer to a greater degree than either Brenda Colvin or Sylvia Crowe. Trained as an architect at the Architectural Association his career since the 1920s has shown enormous diversity, ranging from architecture, town planning and landscape architecture to pure garden design. He has always been guided by a firm belief that landscape architecture is the basis of all the arts and a strongly humanist approach that the primary consideration is the relationship between man and the landscape—be it a private garden or a new town. His ideas were set out in *The Landscape of Man*, which he produced with his wife, Susan Jellicoe, and published in 1975. It is one of the most far-reaching books ever produced about the history of garden design and the study of landscape. This he followed with *The Guelph Lectures on Landscape Design* (1983), in which the titles of the four lectures outline what are for Jellicoe the fundamentals of landscape design: 'Creative Conservation', 'The Creative Subconscious in Landscape Design', 'Space/Time in Landscape Design', and 'Towards a Landscape of Humanism'. Through the connection established with Ronald and Nancy Tree when he worked for them at Ditchley Park before the war, in 1970 Jellicoe was asked by

48

Hidcote Manor. A view across some of the garden's enclosures.

Hidcote Manor. Looking from the Red Borders towards one of the garden's twin gazebos.

East Lambrook. Characteristic mixed planting.

Westonbirt. Euonymus providing autumn colour.

Shute House. The water garden and rill.

Shute House. One of the large box-edged squares of mixed planting.

Sutton Place. Domes of yew leading up to the south front.

Sutton Place. The Swimming-Pool Garden.

Shute House. One of Geoffrey Jellicoe's wooden balconies overlooking the formal canal—an idea he was to use again at Sutton Place.

their son Michael Tree and his wife Lady Anne (a daughter of the tenth Duke of Devonshire) to help with an ambitious replanning of the garden of Shute House, Donhead St Mary in Wiltshire. The Trees had recently moved to Shute House from the Palladian villa of Mereworth Castle in Kent. The garden at Shute is the work of an immensely productive three-way partnership between Jellicoe, the designer, Michael Tree, a painter, and Anne Tree, a knowledgeable plantswoman. The garden reveals the talents of all three in what Jellicoe considers the best professional-client tradition.

'Laura and I drove to luncheon with the Sykeses at Donhead St Mary—our first visit. A solid imposing house on the village street.'[5] Evelyn Waugh's somewhat dismissive mention of his first visit to the home of his future biographer, Christopher Sykes, emphasizes indirectly how, hidden as it is from the street, much of the garden's character derives from the surrounding Wiltshire landscape. Most propitious, however, of the site's natural advantages is the abundant water, which has been capitalized upon to provide many of the outstanding features. In one dark, grotto-like corner a deep, constantly bubbling pool marks the source springs of the River Nadder, and hence the water flows through pools and streams, dispersing across the garden along two main courses.

This main area of the garden is hidden away from the house and approached from lawns on the south side and underneath an apple arch set in the boundary wall. From here one is constantly aware of the sound and sight of water which gives the garden so much of its *raison d'être*. Although the basic pattern of ponds and streams existed before the arrival of the Trees, much of the area was a densely wooded jungle. After judicious clearing one of the most important new features was the channelling of the water to flow downhill in a narrow rill. The water falls in a series of cascades over copper Vs which accentuate the sound and, theoretically, represent treble, alto, tenor and bass chords.

From the top a sheltered terrace looks down upon the descending levels of this water garden. In the uppermost half the water is crossed by three simple stone bridges and, on both sides, lush planting of aquatic plants mix with old-fashioned roses and lilies. Flanking paths are spanned by arches draped with wisteria. Below, the mood changes dramatically and the water descends in sepulchral silence along the narrow rill which leads to three descending formal pools, one square, the other two octagonal. In contrast to the exuberant planting above, here the rill has chaste grass banks on both sides. The inspiration is from the Mogul gardens of Kashmir, which also provided the idea for the bubble fountains in each of the pools all of which are fed by gravity and whence the water bubbles constantly, but quietly, just disturbing the surface. The vista ends at the bottom with a classical statue brought from Mereworth.

This water garden is Shute's most ingenious feature, but it is only one part of a whole eclectic picture that is full of variety while maintaining constant sympathy with the natural surroundings. The formal main flower garden, planted by Lady Anne, comprises six large box-edged squares filled with a mixture of summer flowers, fruit and vegetables. This leads to contrasting areas of shrubberies around two natural pools and, through a beech hedge, to the unexpected discovery of a long formal canal viewed from wooden balconies, cut into the hedge on one side, designed by Jellicoe. At one end the canal is terminated by classical grottoes inspired by William Kent and above, on a grass bank, figures which recall Lady Anne's family-past in that they are copies of figures at Chiswick House, once owned by the Devonshires.

In 1980 Jellicoe was commissioned by Stanley Seegar, a reclusive American millionaire, to redesign the gardens around Sutton Place in Surrey, which Seegar had recently purchased. For Jellicoe the project was to be, 'a consummation of all the work that I have ever done'.[6] In more general terms it is probably the most ambitious post-war garden landscape made for a private individual. Throughout his career Jellicoe had been working more and more towards trying to create gardens which, far from just restoring the past, were sympathetic with their historical surroundings. At a very early stage he appreciated that this was what Seegar hoped to do at Sutton Place. 'I realized he would not be trying to restore the historical gardens (which I'm not interested in doing in the least), but would be trying to create a garden which expresses the modern mind, sympathetic to the ethos of the place, which comprehends the past, the present and the future—considering a landscape design as a continuum and not as a restoration of the past.'[7] He also rapidly appreciated the scale Seegar was thinking of: 'a total composition' as Seegar described it. Jellicoe recalls that shortly after their first meeting he received an inquiry from Sutton Place about whether he could estimate his expected costs. Replying vaguely, 'A lot', Jellicoe was thinking in terms of one or two hundred thousand pounds. The immediate reply was, 'How much? One million, two million, or more?'[8]

Before being commissioned by Seegar, Jellicoe had long been working around the idea that all landscape originates in the human subconscious. Sutton Place provided a sufficiently expansive canvas and sympathetic client for him to put his ideas into practice. It is a complex idea which takes gardens beyond design and lay-out, plants and ornaments, and into the realms of

Sutton Place. Ben Nicholson's dramatic marble wall—the most important piece of architecture in the garden.

abstract modern art. 'The whole concept of Sutton Place is that of duality; one visible world that people see and enjoy—what I call the figurative side of art. The other is the notion of the abstract which I hope hits people maybe some days after they've been here—a very different level of experience which I think is the object of art.'[9] The visual appreciation is easy. Far more difficult is to follow Jellicoe into the sphere of the subconscious and understand that, 'the landscape of Sutton Place is of the mind as well as the eye.'[10]

Jellicoe decided that the evocative Tudor mansion and framework of existing gardens—largely the creation of Lady Northcliffe, wife of the newspaper magnate, carried out around 1900—called for a grand classical scheme. He planned the gardens as an allegory on human life. Creation is represented by a twelve-acre lake which was dug to the north of the house, overcoming the problem that the source of water—from the River Wey—was much lower than the proposed site. In the end it worked, but not without anxious moments. As they were standing together one day watching the lake being dug Jellicoe remarked to Seegar, 'I hope it will be OK,' to which the American replied calmly, 'Don't worry. If it isn't we'll fill it in.'[11]

The main area of gardens, on the east, west and south sides of the house, represent human life. Here the pure garden design is most evident, as well as the planting which, as in many of Jellicoe's gardens, was drawn up by his wife Susan. The gardens are planned to be revealed in a circuit beginning on the east side of the house, where a new walled garden was built to match the existing one to the west.

From the east front of the house stepping-stones lead hazardously across the lily moat to the Paradise Garden. Along the moat are balconies revealing almost certain descent from those at Shute. In the Paradise Garden paths wind between bowers covered by roses, clematis and jasmine with, in the centre of each, a fountain. Along either side are paths spanned by arches of laburnum and honeysuckle. The Paradise Garden leads either to the Secret Garden beyond or to the huge terrace stretching away across the south front of the house. Here, at one end, is a new octagonal gazebo, and pleached limes—a hallmark of Jellicoe's work in many gardens—stretch across part of the paved path along the terrace. Beneath the wall which encloses the Paradise Garden is a deep herbaceous border. Sheltering in front of the house is the intimate Impressionist Garden, filled with bright poppies, penstemons, lilies and other summer flowers which provide the perfect contrast to the clipped yews marching away from the house across the expanse of lawn to the south.

At the far end of the south terrace is the Surrealist Garden, inspired by the painter Magritte, where five great Roman urns on one side lead to a delicate magnolia and an opening in the brick wall at the far end. In the original walled garden, to the east of the house, is the Swimming Pool Garden with numerous stepping-stones leading out to a floating raft. Here one sees clearly the

52

juxtaposition of the garden's modern design and traditional planting with old-fashioned roses in beds around the pool.

The climax of the gardens is the Nicholson Wall. Representing the transformation from life to aspiration, it is positioned at one end of an existing, formal lily pool. The huge wall of white Carrara marble, with its simple geometric pattern of rectangles and circles, is an extraordinarily powerful creation. The artist, Ben Nicholson, a friend of Jellicoe's, had long fostered an ambition to make such a wall sculpture and Jellicoe had often helped him in the search for a suitable site and a sufficiently rich and adventurous patron—whom they eventually found in Stanley Seegar. It was tragic that Nicholson should die before the wall was finally erected. Much of the mystery of Sutton Place's gardens is reflected in Nicholson's comment about his wall. 'You know, it is interesting that had the smaller circles been two inches higher, the design would have been without meaning.' When asked what he meant by meaning he replied, 'How should I know?'[12]

For a few years before the Second World War Jellicoe had been in partnership with Russell Page who, although he did little garden design in Britain after the war and preferred to pursue an international career based in France, was one of the most highly regarded professionals in the world until his death in 1985. As much as to his practical work as a designer this was due to his book, *The Education of a Gardener*, published in 1962, which sets out his ideas on garden design in an inimitable manner. It has become one of the most influential garden books to be published since the war. Its relevance and impact derives from its studies and discussions of the factors and problems influencing contemporary garden making. The impeccable language combines Page's personal philosophy of garden design with illuminating schemes and suggestions for most gardening eventualities. Throughout the book, the author's recurring priority is simplicity:

> All the good gardens I have ever seen, all the garden scenes that have left me satisfied were the result of just such reticence; a simple idea developed just as far as it could be . . . a lovely or impressive site is apt to tempt a garden designer, make him elaborate his plans and work out sumptuous schemes to match his setting. In such cases he would usually do better to discipline any tendancy towards exuberance and let the site tell its own story.[13]

During the 1930s Russell Page was commissioned by the Marquess of Bath to help replan parts of the park and gardens at Longleat House. It was partly this connection and friendship which led him, many years later, to probably the most delightful of his few garden designs in Britain—at the Cottage, Badminton, for Lord Bath's daughter, Lady Caroline Somerset (now the Duchess of Beaufort). Russell Page's skill and Lady Caroline's gardening knowledge and

The Cottage, Badminton. Russell Page's influence is evident in the design of this doorway and the view beyond.

enthusiasm ensured that this would be a most productive partnership and the garden achieved the enviable distinction of being both individual and in the best English tradition, as was remarked upon by John Sales: 'The strong formal outline bounded by hedges and climber-covered walls; the clever variety of intimate enclosures; the wide range of plants used at the same time; it is all here, a worthy development of the Hidcote style and a rare achievement in every way.'[14] While most of the planting was Lady Caroline's work, Russell Page's contribution was mainly in the structure of formal axes linking different parts of the garden, the widespread use of clipped box-edging and some of the garden's ornamental features—notably the white-painted trellised rose arbour in the centre of the French-style potager.

Russell Page's career shows how many landscape architects and garden designers have become international and mix work for private and commercial clients. One of Page's last and largest commissions was the landscaped park around the Pepsi-Cola offices in New York. More than any other designer he also showed to what an extent professionals have been important and influential not only through the gardens they have designed, but also through the books they have written. The title of his book *The Education of a Gardener* may describe his own process of learning, but over the years it has also educated many thousand potential garden-makers. In a tribute in *Country Life*, Fred Whitsey wrote: 'Gardens may go faster than they come, but if this man's gardens all disappear, then the thought that underlay them remains imperishable in his one book, one of the most eloquent in all gardening literature.'[15]

Although few professionals have achieved such a reputation as Russell Page, a number have found time to produce books that, as well as expressing their own ideas, have often had a widespread influence. One of the most productive in recent years has been John Brookes who, after a number of books aimed at owners of small gardens, published, in 1984, *A Place in the Country*. Brookes's training as an assistant to both Brenda Colvin and Sylvia Crowe is evident in his writing and work as a designer, in his concern for the individual qualities of any site and the importance of the surrounding landscape in the creation of a garden.

Brookes runs a successful school of garden design at Denmans, Fontwell, in Sussex. The garden at Denmans has been created over the last forty years by Mrs J.H. Robinson from what was an intensive market garden. In recent years Brookes has been involved in the design and planting of various parts of the garden and, out of all the gardens he has worked in, Denmans perhaps most clearly reveals some of his principles and ideas. Both he and Mrs Robinson show at Denmans their belief that plants should be grouped for their form and texture as much as for colour, and used in relation with hard features—such as gravel, which they have used extensively instead of grass, partly because of its low maintenance demands. Denmans also displays Brookes's view that a garden should be in some aspects an outside room, closely linked to the interior of the house, and he advocates flowing lines in place of a more geometric plan.

If landscape architecture is the modern and expanding cradle of garden design today, longer established, though now declining in comparison, is the background of nurseries. Two of today's most senior figures, James Russell and Graham Stuart Thomas, were for many years partners in Sunningdale Nurseries whose reputation they restored during the 1950s and 1960s. Vernon Russell Smith, who was an assistant at Sunningdale before going on to establish his own practice as a designer, maintains that at one time during the 1960s Russell and Thomas, along with Lanning Roper—gardening correspondent of the *Sunday Times* as well as being a designer—were responsible for the majority of important gardens in England.[16] This was partly because by this

The Temple Garden at Cholmondeley Castle, where James Russell was extensively involved in new designs and planting.

time Thomas had become Gardens Adviser to the National Trust, while also being involved in a number of private gardens such as Sezincote in Gloucestershire.

Thomas's influence is based on his considerable knowledge as a plantsman, one aspect of which has been his pioneering of the revival of old shrub roses. It was largely through his initiation that, in the 1970s, the National Trust decided to establish a garden of old roses at Mottisfont Abbey in Hampshire, many of the plants for which came from Thomas's own collection.

While he was at Sunningdale James Russell was involved in the design of a great number of private gardens, partly because—as nurserymen have often found—it was a natural extension of supplying the plants. Much of his work was overcoming the damage of the war years. 'After the war there were, of course, huge opportunities, total neglect had ruined many large estates and there was the question of replanting on some considerable scale.'[17] Two gardens where he was involved over a number of years were Seaton Delavel in

Northumberland where he laid out an extensive box-edged parterre for Lord Hastings on one side of Vanbrugh's great house, and Cholmondeley Castle where he helped the Marquess and Marchioness of Cholmondeley to recreate many parts of the extensive gardens with plantings of ornamental trees and shrubs. In 1968 he sold Sunningdale Nurseries and moved his stock of plants to Castle Howard in Yorkshire. Here he has established a rose garden in the old walled garden on a similar scale to the one at Mottisfont, as well as planting a large woodland garden and arboretum.

Vernon Russell Smith's career as a designer also originated from his work at Sunningdale Nurseries. It has involved advice at different levels from small-scale planting schemes to complete new lay-outs. Over the years he has detected a number of characteristics in gardens, some of which are clearly the result of labour considerations; the extensive use of groundcover plants, the planting of mixed borders containing annuals, perennials and shrubs as opposed to exclusively herbaceous plants, and leaving large areas of grass rough mown—which is more suitable to modern tractor mowers, enables bulbs to be grown in the grass and minimizes the need for immaculate lawn care which is time-consuming and expensive. Probably the most interesting garden he has worked on in recent years is Toddington Manor in Bedfordshire, where both the house and garden site were in a state of neglect when bought by Sir Neville and Lady Bowman-Shaw in 1979. Since then the garden has been completely replanned, retaining the old walled garden which had to be extensively restored. As well as new rose and herb gardens there is a nut walk and a long pleached lime walk, and large quantities of new trees and spring bulbs.

Lanning Roper, who died in 1983, had a very different background from any of these three, having been born and educated in the United States. He came to England after the war and his career included being a prolific garden journalist —principally as the *Sunday Times* gardening correspondent from 1951 to 1975. His involvement with many gardens was as a consultant, or limited to suggesting planting schemes. In all his work he revealed an instinctive feel for plants and for their arrangement. At Coniston Cold, near Skipton in Yorkshire, he worked for Mr and Mrs Michael Bannister on a garden of unusual interest in that it was planned around the new country house they built in the 1970s. One of the great successes of the garden is the way it maximizes a superb position overlooking a lake. Originally the view was largely obscured by densely planted trees. These have been cleared, leaving a few outstanding specimens, and now a simple grass bank slopes down to the water in a manner sympathetic to both the neo-Georgian house and the surrounding parkland.

Parts of the rest of the garden have been cleverly planned to mark the outline of the much larger Victorian house demolished to make way for the more manageable new one. This has been done by retaining or rebuilding some walls and in the careful positioning of shrub and flower borders. Most dramatic is the retention of the six fluted Doric columns and their entablature from the portico of the old house.

Hillbarn House, in the village of Great Bedwyn in Wiltshire, is the garden where Lanning Roper's work is possibly best revealed and one where the design and planting is predominantly his. It shows how well he used a formal structure, provided by paths and clipped hedges, with balanced planting. The garden throughout reveals a neatness and precision which often characterized Roper's work and which has been carefully retained by Mr and Mrs Andrew Buchanan, who purchased Hillbarn House in 1971 from Lord and Lady Bruntisfield, who had originally commissioned Lanning Roper.

When the Bruntisfields came to Hillbarn in 1962 they were able to purchase an adjoining piece of land and make the originally L-shaped garden into a rectangle. Linking the old and new areas is a path covered by a tunnel of hornbeam leading to a hornbeam arbour. On one side 'windows' in the hornbeam overlook the swimming pool which has been made in the sunken

Hillbarn House. The neat formality of gravel, flowerbeds and clipped hedges often characterized the work of Lanning Roper.

courtyard. Along one side of the new area a gravel path leads, beneath a series of metal arches covered with espalier pears, to Roper's best feature in the garden, a split-level hornbeam hedge and deep border screening the tennis court. The first hedge stretches from the ground to about eight feet high and conceals a gravel path and the border, behind which is the 'aerial' second hedge which has its lower trunks bare and stretches up to conceal all of the fence surrounding the tennis court. In the border Roper used bold clumps of plants such as shrub roses, day-lilies, peonies and agapanthus with spreading grey-leafed plants beneath.

If the majority of today's professional garden designers accept the necessity to mix work for private clients with commercial or institutional ones—and are usually happy to do so—some, like Anthony du Gard Pasley, have always preferred private commissions. Pasley's training and background combine both landscape architecture and nursery work; a pupil of Brenda Colvin, he became resident landscape designer for the well-known nursery firm of R.W. Wallace of Tunbridge Wells and then assistant to Sylvia Crowe before setting up his own practice in 1970. Pasley has tended to work within a fairly localized area in Kent and Sussex.

It was while he was working with Wallace's, during the 1950s, that Pasley became closely involved in the creation of the garden at The Postern, near Tonbridge (see chapter 4). Wallace's had been called in as contractors for the proposed new garden by John Phillimore (a cousin of the architect Claud Phillimore), who had recently bought the house, and as a result the design work was given to Pasley. Phillimore was an ambitious and enthusiastic client and the qualities of the garden which evolved from his partnership with Pasley have been widely recognized. In an article in *Country Life* Arthur Hellyer wrote: 'Though post-war gardens have tended to be smaller than those made before 1939, there have been a great many of them, and some are as good of their kind as any we have seen at any time. One such is The Postern, about a mile to the east of Tonbridge.'[18]

Pasley's contribution at The Postern was to design the extremely successful lay-out that gives the garden its overall structure of enclosures, lawns, hedges, paths and vistas, as well as to give advice on the planting—although, as he himself says, much of this changed and developed with Phillimore's increasing involvement. Very different was his more recent commission to redesign gardens for an amazing modern country house built by John Outram at Wadhurst Park. Pasley is still working here for the owners, Dr and Mrs Rausing, and his main challenge is to create a garden suitable in both scale and character to the extraordinary house and the superb parkland setting which it overlooks from a hilltop position. One intriguing part of the work is the planting of the 1870s winter garden which has been retained from the original Victorian mansion and completely restored.

Wadhurst Park, a garden designed by Anthony du Gard Pasley.

The contrast between The Postern and Wadhurst Park is illustrative of the similar, yet utterly different and individual problems that a professional designer has to face. There is no doubt that, since the Second World War, their work has at times been frustrated by financial considerations: perhaps a client is not able to commission a scheme in its entirety as originally proposed by a designer, or is unwilling for a project to be given what the designer sees as the necessary final stages for satisfactory completion. These are, however, inevitable hazards. There are also professionals who feel that progress in British garden design is impeded by the blinkered, traditionalist views of many potential clients, an attitude which is both unreasonable and fails to grasp the reality of what stirs enthusiasm for gardens in most people today.

Professional designers have been most successful where, rather than imposing their ideas upon clients, mystifying them with complicated planting schemes or dazzling them with expensive architectural projects, they have established an understanding working relationship. Then they are able to use their experience and knowledge to guide a client towards expressing his own ideas, at the same time as creating a garden of originality and character which, as the years pass, he will be able to manage and develop.

PART II
THE GARDENS

4
MAINSTREAM: IN THE HIDCOTE TRADITION

'The immense influence of Hidcote on gardens of this century is manifest both here and abroad . . . Indeed it is difficult to find a country house garden where his [Lawrence Johnston's] ideas have not been used, consciously or unconsciously.'[1] So wrote John Sales in *West Country Gardens* referring to the influence that Hidcote has had in establishing and disseminating a style, a pattern, a formula even for country-house gardens created since the Second World War. There were other gardens in that mould which either survived the Second World War or have been successfully restored since; notably, of course, Sissinghurst. On a smaller scale was Tintinhull, in Somerset, created between the wars by Phyllis Reiss, who had previously lived close to Hidcote in Gloucestershire. Far larger, extending to twenty-five acres, is Newby Hall in Yorkshire, created by Major Edward Compton from 1923 and greatly restored by his son after the war.

For most aspiring gardeners ideas gleaned from elsewhere are often as described by John Phillimore, 'an amalgam of inspiration from visiting other people's gardens'. Few would claim such unsullied originality as did the designer Percy Cane who, when asked who had most influenced him when young, replied curtly that no one had. 'My ideas are wholly my own.'[2]

At The Postern Phillimore had the focus of a charming red-brick house, built in 1757, around which to plan his garden. Other than a small stream flowing along the bottom of the slope in front of the west (entrance) side of the house there was little else of any help and the shape of the site determined that the main areas of garden would be to the east and south. 'Our predecessors were definitely not gardeners. We did not inherit a single shrub or tree worthy of mention, one of the main features being a row of mildewed Dorothy Perkins roses on pillars linked by ropes.'[3] One problem was that the house had been built into a bank so that to the east the ground sloped sharply uphill and the garden could only be seen from the bedroom windows. Outside the drawing-room on the south side of the house the view was blocked by shrubberies.

The problem was alleviated by making a paved terrace along the east front and, on the south-east corner, a flight of generously wide flagged steps to lead down to a much wider terrace along the south front, linking the house to an open lawn. This opened up the view from the house and, at the same time, back from the high bank immediately to one side of the south lawn. Immediately beyond the bank a decaying orchard was replaced with an arboretum of many fine specimens underplanted with daffodils and other bulbs, thus providing a spring garden and an area of informality in a garden of predominant formality. Among the trees are a number which have become popular and fashionable since the war: some of the more recherché prunus and acers such as *P. serrula tibetica* and *A. brilliantissimum*, catalpas—both green and golden, *Gleditsia triancanthos* 'Sunburst', and a tulip tree, as well as one or two more unusual and challenging ones such as *Koelreuteria paniculata*.

The main gardens are a series of geometrically arranged areas enclosed by hedges and linked by paths and vistas. Certainly the hedges—of yew, hornbeam, beech and copper beech—are outstanding and a vital part of the garden's structure and character, be it the yew surrounding the formal rose garden or tall copper beech flanking one long path.

To the east of the house a grass bank rises up from the terrace to a wide lawn which narrows to be flanked by mixed borders backed by yew hedges. The borders lead to a pavilion with trellised pillars and a pediment, designed by

The Postern. A view of the house from the pavilion designed by John Phillimore.

The Cottage, Badminton. The garden from the windows of the house.

Mottisfont Abbey. The rose garden.

Hillbarn House. The pear arches and box-edged path designed by Lanning Roper.

The Postern. Looking along the rose walk with generous clumps of
catmint spilling out on to the gravel path.

The Postern. One of a pair of stone cherubs with the pink rose 'Bantry Bay'
trained over the wooden arbour and, to the left, 'Paul's Scarlet Climber'.

Jenkyn Place. A view through a yew arch across the double herbaceous
borders to the Sundial Garden on the far side.

Bradenham Hall. A formal vista between clipped yew and the garden's
main herbaceous border to a classical statue at the top.

Phillimore himself, which, as well as providing the focal point for this main view, plays a dual role that enhances the fluidity of the garden's composition. On the far side of the pavilion, french doors open on to the garden's cross-axis of a pleached lime walk that screens the tennis court beyond. As well as the tennis court a swimming pool has been well placed on this far side of the garden and both are incorporated into the garden's overall structure by hedges which divide and surround them and the more decorative planting such as the hedge of floribunda roses along the front of the pool and the mixed shrub border behind the tennis court, which marks the garden's perimeter on this side.

In one direction the pleached lime walk leads to columnar yews and a rose walk beyond where individual old-fashioned shrub roses alternate with ramblers cascading off tripods. At the far end wrought-iron gates mark the garden's boundary on this side while retaining the view out to orchards beyond. At the other end the focal point of the lime walk is one of the garden's many fine pieces of statuary, a marble figure of Bacchus and an acolyte.

The garden's four enclosures lie two on each side of the main lawn and borders leading to the pavilion. The largest is the formal rose garden that—although striking with tall yew hedges, fine statues of Ceres and Proserpine, urns and paved steps and paths—is the least original part of the garden and reminiscent of a good pre-war country-house sunken rose garden, with its rectangular beds of hybrid teas. The statues were purchased in Venice in the 1950s when it was still possible to export works of art from Italy and reasonably cheap to do so. The statues cost less than £100 each and two stone benches from the same place cost £125 each—including packing and transport.

Behind the statues, narrow openings in the yew hedges lead to the more refreshing and intimate Roman Garden where a wooden pergola, draped with climbing roses and clematis, covers a raised walk with cherub figures at both ends. The walk extends along two sides of this garden, the main area of which is a pattern of paving stones and cobbles surrounding a formal diamond of low, purple berberis hedges enclosing Hidcote lavender and a stone urn. The two other enclosures are the Magnolia Garden, the original trees of which have been replaced by simple brick-edged flower-beds, and what was the children's garden, now planted mainly with camellias although a delightful miniature summer-house recalls its earlier purpose.

Beyond the entrance front of the house the garden is kept simple with lawn sloping down to the small stream crossed by a rustic wooden bridge. To one side of the lawn is a further variety of ornamental trees, including a ginkgo and the striking *Gleditsia triancanthos* 'Sunburst'. As is often the case in young gardens the collection of ornamental trees at The Postern helps as much as anything else to give a feeling of established maturity. Either planted individually on open lawn or together, as in the old orchard, they are the ideal foil to the more closely planted areas of the enclosures.

The Postern. One of a pair of cherub statues in the formal Roman Garden. Behind is the copper beech of one of the garden's many hedges; to the left is the rambling rose 'Adelaide d'Orleans', to the right the clematis 'Mme. le Coultre' (Marie Boisselot).

The theme of enclosures is the backbone of the garden at Jenkyn Place, Bentley, Hampshire which Major and Mrs Gerald Coke have created steadily through the post-war decades. As they recorded:

We came here in 1941 and, of course, could do nothing to alter the garden until the war had been over for two or three years. In fact, as one might expect, things got worse after our arrival; nearly all the lawns went for hay; there were cattle in the field which is now the lower part of the garden; and we concentrated on growing fruit and vegetables rather than flowers and shrubs. But it gave us time to think, time to live with the garden and to imagine some of the changes we would make when it became possible to do so—and to reject most of our original ideas. We did not consciously evolve an overall plan to which we have stuck ever since. Far from it; new ideas are still being given practical shape and the garden is changing all the time. But as a background to all our planning and as a guide in the realization of our concepts we have adopted certain principles. First, because we live here all the year round, the garden must present different and interesting faces at all seasons; secondly, a garden must not disclose all its secrets at first sight, it must have rooms, like a house, which each have their own special character but are at the same time a part of the whole;

thirdly, we must make use of our good soil and aspect by growing some plants which are half-hardy, even a little exotic; fourthly, shrubs need space to breathe, not so much literally as in the context of their surroundings . . . finally, and perhaps self-evidently, we must design the garden to save labour.[4]

The Cokes inherited the remnants of an Edwardian garden, in particular some yew hedges immediately to the south-west of the house, invaluable mature trees which protected the boundaries of most areas of the proposed garden and a site sloping south-east towards the River Wey, with a soil of upper greensand. The proposals for the new garden immediately extended well beyond the limits of the old one and at the time of writing there were seventeen principal areas, each with its own name, character and appearance. The gardens are planned so that there is a natural progression from the smaller, more formal enclosures closest to the house through the areas beyond linked by lawns and grass paths to the far end. From here the main vista stretches back to the house for over 250 yards, across immaculate lawn and between individual trees and shrubs. To maintain unity over such a large area has been as much of an achievement for the Cokes as the seemingly limitless variety of plants which they have incorporated throughout. It is partly achieved by a balance between the

Jenkyn Place. The Sundial Garden, enclosed by yew hedges, and entered on both sides through elegant wrought-iron gates.

enclosed areas and firm axes and the expert use of paved and brick paths, steps and gateways and enticing openings in hedges, leading from one part of the gardens to the next.

The scale varies from the small and intimate, as in the Dutch Garden enclosed on three sides by old farm buildings, to grand planting, notably in the double herbaceous borders, backed by tall yew hedges which stretch from the wrought-iron gates at one end to a stone seat backed by curving clipped yew. Even within the confined space of the Dutch Garden—which the visitor comes to first—the quantity and variety of plants give a taste of what the rest of the gardens have in store: climbing roses and the scented *Trachelospermum jasminoides* on the walls, tree peonies and cistus, a bed devoted to *Daphne collina*, to name but a small selection. Next door, in the Sundial Garden, one also comes across the sort of contrast that is evident throughout: a paved area given over to pots filled mainly with scented pelargoniums and enclosed by yew hedges, with beautiful peacock pattern wrought-iron gates on both sides. In one direction a paved path leads out of the Sundial Garden to the bowling green and rose garden.

In the other direction the path leads to the herbaceous borders running at right angles. Immediately beyond, and parallel, is the Long Walk with, stretching along one side, a raised rock border and, on the other, espalier fruit trees which conceal three rectangular areas next to each other; the Italian Garden, the old-fashioned rose garden and the Yew Garden. These are divided by three paths: two apple walks, one underplanted with crinums, the other with alpine strawberries, and a path between peony borders. Beyond is the Herb Garden, unusual in its circular shape and surrounding espalier cider apple trees and centring on a fine marble eighteenth-century copy of Giambologna's statue of Bacchus, next the Leaf Garden with a mixture of trees and shrubs and a stress on foliage, and the gloriously named Armillary Sphere Garden, an area of seventeenth-century formality that has as its centrepiece 'the skeleton celestial globe of metal rings representing the equator and the tropics'. Here the four individual trees planted in the centre of square lawns divided by herringbone-patterned brick paths reflect the careful selection which the Cokes have applied to all their planting: a white mulberry, a date plum, a medlar and *Prunus serrula*, with polished mahogany bark.

The furthest feature of the gardens is the Lion Walk, an ideally rewarding vista between tapestry hedges of green and copper beech to a slumbering, life-size stone lion at the far end. From here, as the gentle progression back to the house begins, through the Lion Garden with shrub roses and sorbus to the Long Valley sweeping majestically up the slope, the visitor has to agree that the Cokes' original aspirations, given that they maintain the garden with the help of three full-time gardeners, have been largely fulfilled.

In contrast to Jenkyn, where the site of the garden is blessed with many

Jenkyn Place. The Lion Walk, a vista at the far end of the garden from the house, where tapestry green and copper beech hedges flank the stretch of grass leading to the recumbent stone figure.

natural advantages, at Bradenham Hall Colonel and Mrs Richard Allhusen, who bought the house and surrounding farmland in 1951, have overcome considerable obstacles in the creation of their garden. Bradenham Hall sits on one of the few hills in Norfolk—in fact the highest in the county—and there hardly seems to be a day in the year when the wind does not blow, usually with great force, from the south-west. In addition the soil is heavy clay over chalk, thereby ruling out the possibility of growing acid-loving plants. Although the attractive house, built in 1750 by Thomas Smythe, has a distinguished literary background, having been the home of both Rider Haggard and L.P. Hartley (for whom it provided the setting of his novel *The Go-Between*), its advantages for a garden were less evident. The courtyard and walled garden to the north of the house were grossly overgrown, woods and undergrowth had encroached relentlessly from the north and east—while the best trees had been felled by marauding timber merchants. On the other side of the house most of what is now garden was park grazed by cattle with railings close to the house.

The Allhusens' work at Bradenham has been on an impressive scale—the gardens cover twenty-seven acres—and it has been carried out with a precision that is evident in the general air of orderliness and the immaculate maintenance. In the early days they were given some advice and assistance by George Taylor of *Country Life* and Frank Knight, then director of the Royal Horticultural Society's garden at Wisley and later managing director of the East Anglian nursery, Notcutts. Otherwise the work is their own and shows their two priorities: building up a collection of trees—Colonel Allhusen's primary interest—and creating a series of sheltered enclosures, where Mrs Allhusen has been responsible for most of the planting.

One of the Allhusens' main achievements has been to capitalize on the house's commanding position and open up extensive views across the wide Norfolk landscape beyond, at the same time as creating parts of the garden on an altogether more intimate and personal scale. The main view is to the south, where the farmland has been pushed back from the house and is contained by a ha-ha, and expansive lawn now slopes away between young trees on either side. It is here, and on either side of the new drive approaching from the south-east, that Colonel Allhusen has planted his formidable collection of trees, which must comprise one of the most extensive arboretums planted since the war. The initial inspiration came from Westonbirt, which the Allhusens used to visit regularly, taking notes of what they liked. Planting began in 1954. Now there are 900 different varieties with all major characteristics represented: flowering trees, autumn foliage, berries and fruit, decorative bark, scent, fastigiate or weeping habit and all shades of coloured foliage—coniferous and deciduous.

All around the trees the second main feature of this extensive part of the gardens are the daffodils, which the Allhusens have been planting continuously—sometimes at a rate of two or three thousand bulbs per year. The daffodils are planted in large groups of single cultivars and the huge carpet of flowers reaches a climax around an old oak where a wide cartwheel has been planted in gently merging segments.

The gardens to the north-west of the house are quite different. Yew hedges were planted, all of which have now attained a height of over ten feet, to create a series of symmetrical enclosures, aligned with gateways into the walled garden on one side and sheltered by the mature woodland which has been steadily pushed back on the other. In one compartment a vista has been made across gently sloping lawn to one of a number of eighteenth-century stone statues which the Allhusens inherited at Bradenham and have judiciously repositioned to provide focal points. To one side of the lawn is a deep herbaceous border, backed by shrubs which, on their other side, flank a narrow path leading to a second statue. This path is called the Philosopher's Walk.

A path breaking the border at right angles leads, in one direction, into the

Bradenham Hall. The Philosopher's Walk, with climbing roses on one side, herbaceous plants on the other and the Philosopher at the end.

walled garden and, in the other, across the lawn, to the main axis of the enclosures; a pleached lime walk, underplanted with daffodils, which has been made on the site of a canker-ridden apple orchard. Along the lime walk an opening to one side leads to the rose garden. Here a catholic mixture of old-fashioned and modern shrub roses has replaced a variety of fruit trees, a few of the healthier apples being retained as hosts for climbing roses. The central grass path widens into two effective circles around an old medlar at one end and at the other a young mulberry *Morus nigra* 'Chelsea', a variety which fruits far sooner than most. On the opposite side of the lime walk is a new paved garden called the Sundial Garden, planned by Mrs Allhusen and replacing beds of floribunda roses. The pattern of paving, brick and cobbles was laid out by Notcutts and in the centre of four brick circles are standard *Salix helvetica* surrounded by helichrysum and artemisia. Beyond here the geometric yew hedges extend to conceal the tennis court and swimming pool in two separate enclosures.

Bradenham reveals how it has been possible since the Second World War to have a large garden which is not labour intensive—thanks to good planning and modern aids. Both Colonel and Mrs Allhusen work continuously in the garden, with the help of one gardener, his wife, and an old-age pensioner. The mowing takes Colonel Allhusen five hours a fortnight on a tractor mower—the tree-planting has been planned to accommodate the sweep of the mower

71

—while the gardener is able to clip all the yew hedges himself, using a mechanical clipper.

Despite its name and imposing eighteenth-century architecture, the Manor House, Bledlow in Buckinghamshire, has also been a farmhouse for much of its life. Parts of the garden created by Lord and Lady Carrington since 1968 lie on the site of old farm buildings. The house has belonged to Lord Carrington's family for nearly two hundred years, but successive tenant farmers have occupied it for much of the time until the Second World War. When the Carringtons came to the house in 1948 there was little of interest in the garden except the enclosed area of the walled kitchen garden to the east of the house. With roads on two sides and farm buildings and fields on the other two, the area of garden has not been extended. Instead, with limited views out it has been planned to make the most of the house's elegant façades and give areas of different, integrated interest on three sides.

The Carringtons gave the garden much of its framework in the years immediately after the war by planting the series of beech and yew hedges which form the major divisions and—perhaps most strikingly—the pleached limes along the drive that approaches from the south-east, where great boxes of clipped branches supported on slender trunks now form a tunnel of leaf in summer. The main impetus for developing the garden did not come, however, until 1967, when a large thirteenth-century barn, which stood immediately to the south of the house, accidentally burnt down.

Although it was a sad loss, the barn's destruction produced considerable relief for it opened up a space between the house and farm buildings which had previously stood uncomfortably close. The decision was immediately taken to develop the site of the barn as a new area of garden and the Carringtons called in the landscape architect Robert Adams to plan and execute a new design, the first of two phases of work he carried out in the garden. Adams proposed treating the area formally, in character with the period (*c.* 1710) of this side of the house, and partly because of the symmetrical rectangular shape of the site which had a splendid seventeenth-century granary set up on a bank and forming the boundary opposite the house. At the same time the opportunity was taken to annex a bit more space from the farm by making a tennis court on the adjoining site of some old cattle-yards.

From the house a path flanked by pairs of *Viburnum carlesii* leads to a square sunken lily pool enclosed by low brick walls and neat beech hedges. Invisible from the ground-floor windows of the house, the pool is an ideal way of using the varied levels of the site. Beyond the pool, steps lead up to a small enclosed terrace, beyond which shrub roses are planted along the grass bank in front of the granary. To one side a path leads from the house to a delightful gazebo with a hipped roof, built as part of the new design. (Here, as with all the brick paths he laid in different parts of the garden, Adams was careful to use old materials.)

72

The Manor House, Bledlow. Clipped yew and box and brick paths surround a central astrolabe in one of the enclosures.

To one side a long border of old-fashioned shrub roses screens the tennis court beyond. On the opposite side of the pool the formality is continued with pleached limes—echoing the older ones along the drive—perched on the top of a small mound.

Having completed this area in 1969 Adams was asked by the Carringtons to redesign the area to the north-east of the house, on one side of the entrance forecourt, to provide a flowing link between the larger areas on each side. It was decided to retain the now well-grown yew hedges and within these Adams devised three intimate, strictly formal enclosures: one with a pattern of clipped box, gravel and brick paths around a central astrolabe; the second with formal box-edged beds containing individual herbs and low herbaceous plants; and the third—and largest—left undivided by low hedging and covered with spreading plants around paved paths, most notably a central carpet of lavender.

The more open appearance of the last of the enclosures gives a subtle introduction to the large area of lawn and mixed borders which lies beyond.

73

Part of the lawn is manicured for croquet and to one side is a well-designed swimming pool and summer-house, enlivened in summer with tubs of fuchsias and pelargoniums. The whole area is informal and relaxing, with philadelphus, lilacs, laburnum and many traditional herbaceous plants filling the various borders.

In front of the house's impressive north-facing façade, although the long-established herbaceous border along one side has been retained—albeit replanted— the creation of a terrace along the house with rectangular beds enclosed by raised bricks and divided by a brick path, has successfully linked house and garden in a manner which Adams clearly recognized to be one of the main priorities of his work. 'Perhaps the major point to arise out of this scheme is that it demonstrates the need for such houses to be not only preserved but given the correct setting and perspective in order to create a total environment; one which fuses house and land together.'[5]

Much of the garden's success stems from the way in which Adams's designs and the framework he has created have been enhanced by the planting carried out by Lady Carrington.

While there are many gardens made since the Second World War which have achieved outstanding—and often surprising—maturity, few, as yet, can be felt to have attained an historical reputation. Thus the national *Register of Parks and Gardens of Special Historic Interest in England*, compiled by the Historic Buildings and Monuments Commission (better known as English Heritage), takes 1939 as its cut-off point. No new gardens made, or garden features added since that date are mentioned. At the same time, there are a selection of gardens that, by virtue of the reputations they have achieved with their contemporaries, have virtually guaranteed themselves a niche in English gardening history for future generations—none more so than Barnsley House in Gloucestershire.

The garden at Barnsley has been made by David and Rosemary Verey, who inherited the house in 1951. It was built of Cotswold stone in 1697 and given its Tudor-Gothic additions in the 1830s. Until his death in 1984 the Vereys were a gardening partnership in the Harold Nicolson–Vita Sackville-West tradition; he was an architect and architectural historian, she a garden historian and plantswoman of increasing skill. His instinctive desire for order and love of the traditions of English vernacular architecture ensured that the garden would have firm lines and architectural ornaments. Her knowledge of plants and their use in the past has been applied to the basic framework. As a result the garden is both the product of two keen and critical minds and a modern garden drawing freely on inspiration from the past.

Although the garden is their creation the Vereys started with encouraging basics: the tall, gabled house as a centrepiece, with a castellated and colonnaded veranda on one end (a legacy from the Reverend Adolphus Musgrave, who made the alterations to the house and was one of successive clergymen

74

who inhabited it from the eighteenth century until the house was bought by David Verey's parents). Stone walls enclosed the south and east sides of the garden with a Gothic alcove in the south-east corner, while there were many mature trees—particularly along the drive. Also Irish yews flanked the paved path crossing the main area of garden from the house.

Rosemary Verey freely admits that she has drawn many ideas from other people's books—in particular *The Education of a Gardener* by Russell Page and various books by Vita Sackville-West, as well as a number of older, especially seventeenth-century, volumes. In front of the castellated veranda is a knot garden with hedges of box and wall germander forming tight diamond patterns in gravel and surrounded by hedges of rosemary with clipped spirals of holly on the corners. Beyond the lawn on this side of the house is a collection of ornamental trees chosen for their flowers or foliage: crabs, cherries and sorbus as well as two metasequoias, a ginkgo, a tulip tree, a catalpa and a *Paulownia tomentosa*. The trees are planted around mown paths cutting through longer grass and bulbs and this area is called the Wilderness as it would have been in the seventeenth century—even if many of the varieties would not have been

Barnsley House. Irish yews flank the paved path leading to the garden front of the house. On the right hand side is the herb garden, just outside the kitchen.

available then. The idea for an ornamental vegetable garden or potager, with symmetrical beds planted between brick paths came partly from Villandry in France, and from *The Country House-wife's Garden*, by William Lawson, first published in 1617. It was not only Lawson's ideas which Rosemary Verey followed, but some of his practical advice: that the beds should not be more than five feet wide to ensure easy weeding. As she said, 'Reading the old books and visiting great gardens made my head swim with ambitious thoughts of combining formality with luxuriance of planting, always trying to remember that every added detail should be a contribution not a distraction.'[6]

The balance between formality and the planting which Rosemary Verey pinpoints recurs constantly throughout the garden at Barnsley, most successfully in the largest area, to the south and east of the house. Deep borders around the edges of the lawns contain a mixture of small trees, shrubs and flowers, seemingly arranged in a random fashion, but grouped with an eye for blending colour and scent, and succession through the seasons. Along the wide paved terrace in front of the house *Alchemilla mollis* spreads across the flagstones, while against the house clematis, roses, honeysuckle and wisteria mix with more unusual wall-plants such as *Fremontodendron californicum*, with its striking yellow flowers. Parallel to the strong axis of the Irish yews a herb garden, planted with a diamond pattern of box hedging, leads naturally away from the kitchen door.

The paved path between the Irish yews leads to one side of the garden where, at right angles, are the garden's two main formal vistas. A Tuscan Doric temple—which originally stood at Fairford Park and was given to David Verey, taken down and re-erected at Barnsley in 1962—stands at one end of the longest vista. From here a succession of features makes up the view right across the garden; in front of the temple a lily pool surrounded by paving and seats made by the Vereys' son Charles. This area is divided from the wide grass walk beyond by wrought-iron railings and gates. Once past the Irish yews and flower borders in front of the house the grass walk is flanked on one side by a deep mixed border and leads finally to a pool and fountain piece of frogs spouting water against a tablet carved into two rams, made for the garden by Simon Verity. Verity also sculpted the statue of a lady in hunting-dress which stands, partly concealed by trees, on the far side of the lawn leading to the Wilderness.

Parallel to this walk is the second vista where pleached limes lead to a cobbled walk beneath a laburnum tunnel, underplanted with tall purple alliums. Although pleached limes and laburnum have become fashionable and widely used since the war, they have rarely been used to such good effect and with such expert precision. The limes are planted the perfect distance apart for the walk between to be secluded without being cramped while, beyond, the span of the laburnum arch is similarly well proportioned.

76

Barnsley House. The veranda on one end of the house, looking onto the Knot Garden, with benches designed by the Vereys' son Charles.

Barnsley House. The plate fitted to the top of a stone pedestal at the end of the laburnum walk, which encapsulates the creation of David and Rosemary Verey at Barnsley.

SIMON VERITY FECIT

As no man be very miserable that is master of a garden here, so will no man ever be happy who is not sure of a garden hereafter... where the first Adam fell the second rose

ROSEMARY VEREY DONAT MCMLXXIII

DAVID VEREY AETAT LX

JOHN EVELYN SCRIPSIT MDCLX

As well as the great variety of plants which the garden contains (within a total area of only three and a half acres), it is the quality of planning and planting exemplified in the lime and laburnum walk that make the garden a notable addition to the tradition it follows. Meanwhile its spirit is encapsulated in a square tablet on the small pillar at the end of the laburnum walk. It was a present from Rosemary Verey to her husband on his sixtieth birthday, carrying a quotation from John Evelyn inscribed by Simon Verity: 'As no man be very miserable that is master of a garden here; so will no man ever be happy who is not sure of a garden hereafter . . . where the first Adam fell the second rose.' It is a singularly appropriate inscription.

Whether the garden at Barnsley will survive and its reputation become historical is uncertain, as it is with all the gardens discussed in this chapter. What is significant at the moment is that these gardens have, in a sense, taken up the mantle of distinguished predecessors and, in their own quite individual ways, established that a certain style of garden as conceived by Lawrence Johnston has become both a central and continuing part of Britain's gardening tradition.

5
THE PERSONAL GARDEN

When Geoffrey Jellicoe laid out the grand parterre garden at Ditchley Park in the 1930s he was largely left to his own devices by Ditchley's owners the Trees. Twenty years later Nancy Tree, who had remarried and become Nancy Lancaster, embarked upon making her own garden at Haseley Court in Oxfordshire, which, compared to Ditchley, was an entirely personal creation. The outstanding Queen Anne house already had its well-known topiary chess garden on one side, which Nancy Lancaster left alone—instead she concentrated her efforts in other areas, in particular the large, rectangular kitchen garden that, in 1955 when she bought it, was a derelict field.

In 1945 Nancy Lancaster had bought Lady Colefax's partnership in Colefax and Fowler and during the ensuing years she achieved a reputation as an undisputed 'arbiter of taste'. As John Martin Robinson commented in *The Latest Country Houses*: 'Mrs Lancaster, together with Lady Colefax and John Fowler, was largely responsible for the evolution of the sophisticated and romantic English Country House Style.'[1] Having already decorated for herself two outstanding country houses—Kelmarsh in Northamptonshire and Ditchley—before the war, she did the same at Haseley, with the significant addition of a new garden which she had herself not attempted at the other houses.

Nancy Lancaster was, by her own admission, no knowledgeable gardener when she started work at Haseley. 'I am not a horticulturalist and delight in a hollyhock in the front and a violet at the back: I like common plants best.'[2] In creating the garden she drew ideas from her childhood in Virginia and from the formal gardens of France and Renaissance Italy, incorporating the more English characteristic of a profusion of traditional flowering plants.

The walled garden was simply divided into four large squares, with an elaborate trellised arbour at the junction of the four main paths. Each square was given its own identity: in one the parterre of Torcello (the pattern of which was taken from Byzantine mosaics on the small island of Torcello in the Lagoon of Venice), with walks of flint cobbles winding between low box hedges enclosing beds of lavender, bergenia, santolina, roses and lilies around standard fruit trees; in the second a simple croquet lawn with four fruit trees trained into the shape of wine goblets. The third square was a formal French potager, with vegetables and flowers used equally for ornament and utility; and in the fourth was a lawn with spirals of topiary on its corners and enclosed by mixed borders. Around two sides paths were originally enclosed by tunnels of pleached limes—later, when they proved unsuccessful, replaced by hornbeam—and the views ended in different ornaments: an urn in one case, a stone grotto in another. In front of the walls of the other two sides of the garden Nancy Lancaster indulged her delight in abundant flowering with deep box-edged borders planted predominantly with old-fashioned roses.

In addition to the kitchen garden, Nancy Lancaster's most successful addition at Haseley was to transform an old fish-pond along one side of the gardens into a formal canal, terminating at one end in a cascade flowing from a stone mask set between flint piers surmounted with stone balls. Beyond the cascade the long vista was further extended in a box-edged path leading to a large urn on the boundary of the garden and the surrounding fields. A path approaching the canal from the house was aligned at right angles across the stretch of water to a fountain flanked by stone figures of a boy and girl.

If much of Nancy Lancaster's design and planting in the kitchen garden at Haseley recall the gardens of her Virginian home where, as she writes herself, 'boxwood was greatly valued, herbaceous borders unknown and flowers and vegetables intermingled',[3] the canal and its vistas hark back to the continental gardens of the sixteenth and seventeenth centuries. Although only ever open for charity, Haseley achieved a considerable reputation; for many people it was a paragon of good taste.

In recent years, however, Nancy Lancaster has moved out of Haseley Court into the neighbouring Coach House which she converted herself. To some extent confirming the melancholy thought that the more personal a garden the more threatened is its survival, her garden has, in parts, deteriorated as she has been unable to tend it, but in its heyday during the 1960s and 1970s, 'sophisticated and romantic' were as applicable to Nancy Lancaster's garden at Haseley as to her quality and style as an interior decorator.

William Lawson's *The Country House-wife's Garden*, published nearly four hundred years ago, was the first book aimed specifically at lady gardeners. Since then the feminine touch has been ever-present in the development of English gardens, but it has not been until the twentieth century that women truly have come into their own. Many of the great gardening figures since 1900—Gertrude Jekyll, Vita Sackville-West and Margery Fish—have been women, of course, whereas in the past they have usually been overwhelmingly male: John Tradescant and John Parkinson in the seventeenth century, William Kent, 'Capability' Brown and Humphry Repton in the eighteenth, and John Loudon, William Nesfield and William Robinson in the nineteenth. Since the Second World War 'the Englishwoman's Garden' has been chronicled in two volumes of a book of that title, and their gardens have become their own

Barnsley House. The temple which came from Fairford Park.

Haseley Court. The walled garden.

The Old Rectory, Burghfield. The stone statue of Antinous rises from the pool at one end of the garden, around which are mixed plants, including azaleas and hostas.

Chilcomb House. Pebbles from nearby Chesil Beach make the paths dividing small squares filled with an abundant mixture of plants.

Chilcomb House. Looking between columnar Irish yews up
the garden's double border.

The Old Rectory, Farnborough. The swimming-pool garden.

Biddick. One of the garden's cross-axes:
clipped beech and yew with classical urns.

Sutton Park. Looking across the main central terrace.

In the sheltered courtyard at the Old Rectory, Burghfield, with an impressive white tree peony dominating the border on one side.

domains; as indeed, have their kitchens. Many of today's outstanding gardeners and cooks are people whose mothers hardly planted a bulb or boiled an egg in their lives.

Geoffrey Jellicoe maintains that a love of flowers, colour and scent is an important feminine instinct, contrasting with a man's predominant desire for an ordered structure. This is the basis of many gardening partnerships—the Nicolsons at Sissinghurst and the Vereys at Barnsley, for example.

In the creation of their garden at the Old Rectory, Burghfield in Berkshire, Esther and Ralph Merton have been in this mould. They bought the red-brick Georgian rectory in 1950, when the garden area was large but virtually empty. In her own words Esther Merton described her initial ambitions and at the same time pointed to the feminine priorities:

> From the very beginning I knew that I wanted to make an 'old' garden full of sweet-smelling cottage plants, aromatic herbs and shrubs, and voluptuous cabbage roses, dripping with enough scent to waft me nostalgically back to my childhood. This would create a proper setting for our eighteenth-century house, with its lovely old pink bricks and inviting feeling of warmth and welcome. It must have been the home of many happy old rectors and their contented calvesfoot-jelly-making wives.[4]

81

Together the Mertons planned the initial lay-out and necessary alterations. The main area of garden stretched away from one side of the house to the largest of three ponds. The ground was levelled to make a gentle slope to the water and yew hedges, sixty yards long, were planted twenty-five feet apart. These were to provide the backing for the garden's main vista of double herbaceous borders. Behind one hedge an area was set aside for a swimming pool, now enclosed on three sides with yew hedges and on the other by a brick wall, with its pillared and porticoed loggia designed by Ralph Merton in partnership with the architect, Claud Phillimore.

Far more than the design, however, it is the plants which are of the primary importance at the Old Rectory and in thirty years the irrepressible Esther Merton has filled the garden with a remarkable selection, both traditional and rare. Her compulsive enthusiasm both for collecting plants—asking for a cutting of a rambler rose from a cottage garden she passed one day or collecting tender miniatures from the Mediterranean—and tending to them, gives the garden a burgeoning appearance through much of the year. The herbaceous borders flower from May until late summer, mainly with a succession of traditional plants. The large pond at the bottom is surrounded by azaleas, rhododendrons and *Acer* 'Senkaki' and most parts of the garden contain a profusion of shrub and climbing roses—trained against walls, up the pillars of the loggia or covering the unsightly roofs of outbuildings.

Esther Merton's enthusiasm for growing traditional plants which are now threatened species is perhaps best shown in the spring garden, and the hellebores and old primroses which are two outstanding features. Elsewhere, a functional backyard is now decorated with a large collection of sinks that contain many of the garden's smaller rare visitors from overseas. As well as the individual qualities of plants, one curving border, containing old-fashioned roses, pastel-shaded herbaceous plants and various wall-plants behind shows successful plant associations which can be found throughout the garden. If the revitalization of an old garden site with new planting of variety and effusive quantity is a characteristic of many post-war gardens, then the Old Rectory at Burghfield is a prime example.

In a comparable manner to the Mertons, who have created a garden which succeeds in retaining the long-established atmosphere of a traditional rectory garden as the basis of their new garden, John and Caryl Hubbard have made a garden at Chilcomb House in Dorset which retains the essential character of an old Dorset farmhouse. The part-sixteenth- and part-seventeenth-century stone farmhouse sits on a south-facing slope above the main area of garden, with views beyond over the open downland which stretches to the coast a mile away.

John Hubbard is a painter, his wife is actively involved in the art world and Chilcomb is an artist's garden. When they moved here, in 1969, virtually all

Chilcomb House. Looking along the top grass terrace is the sloping walled garden, with the tiny church at the end, and the old-fashioned rose 'Fantin-Latour' in flower in the foreground.

planting in the garden had disappeared, but its basic rectangular shape with boundary walls had survived—and probably changed little during the three hundred years since the house had been built, when the garden had been tended by successive farmers and their wives. Repairing broken walls and steps, the Hubbards have left the garden's old structure undisturbed and created further subdivisions so that the garden is planned round four smaller squares.

For John Hubbard the most important factors in the garden are the interplay of the regular spaces of the garden with those of the house above, which they reflect, and the blending colour and form of plants. Traditional herbaceous plants, mixing freely with shrubs, old-fashioned roses and herbs create the atmosphere of an ideal cottage or farmhouse garden with an ease which disguises the skill in planting. The lower two squares of the garden are given over to an orchard, where some old apple trees have been kept and are now hosts to rambling roses such as 'Seagull', while the rough grass beneath is filled with bulbs, and a vegetable potager planted in a style the Hubbards saw in many French country gardens: with different ornamental lettuces edging rows of onion, beetroot and herbs all mixed with clumps of sweet peas, small summer flowers and standard gooseberries.

The main division across the garden's slope is a grass walk between tapestry hedges of green and copper beech, holly and yew, the upper hedge stretching the full width of the garden, the lower one half way, allowing an open view into the orchard from the path. In the centre the crossing of the two main paths is marked by three fastigiate yews and above here are the two main borders filled with old shrub roses, herbaceous plants and annuals whose shades are blends of pink, blue, mauve and white. To one side, part of the garden has been subdivided into square beds by paths made out of pebbles from nearby Chesil Beach and the beds planted with traditional plants—aquilegia, columbines, ranunculus and penstemon, as well as taller lilies and clumps of herbs and some vegetables. Enclosing screens of espalier apples and pears, mixing with clematis and roses, have been made both here and on the far side of the main central borders, where a small lawn surrounds a sundial—one of the garden's few ornaments.

Roses are a principal feature of the garden; at one end a path leading up the slope to a small flight of steps between massive Irish yews, is covered by a simple wooden pergola over which are trained 'Bleu Magenta', 'Francis E. Lester', 'Mme Alice Garnier' and 'Félicité et Perpétue'. A grass terrace along the top of the walled garden, which was originally completely concealed when the Hubbards arrived, has domes of 'Fantin-Latour' along one side and stretches round to form an L, where the white rose 'Alba Céleste' over a wooden arbour contrasts with the brilliant red 'Crimson Conquest' on the wall nearby.

In their unpretentious use of traditional as well as more unusual plants and success in creating a garden which is both clearly individual and harmonious with its simple origins and surroundings, John and Caryl Hubbard have achieved what has become for many people a gardening ideal. In the popular imagination the quintessential English garden would surely be something akin to Chilcomb House.

In sharp contrast to Chilcomb House, a painter's garden, the use of plants is of secondary importance to the architectural features for the distinguished sculptor, Arnold Machin (whose work includes the designs for many recent currency issues such as the decimal coins). Machin spent many years making a garden at Offley Rock, in Staffordshire. In 1979 he moved to nearby Garmelow Manor where, with the help of his son Francis, an architect who has enjoyed considerable success with the Gothic conservatories he designs and markets, he has created a new garden that, in reduced size, harks back to the eighteenth-century landscapes.

Much of the garden has been planned within the large farmyard to one side of the house, enclosed on all sides by marvellous barns built of vivid red local brick. Arnold Machin has brought in a collection of urns, statues and busts and arranged them in different parts of the farmyard, at the same time as converting some old pig-sties into a small enclosed garden. The most adventurous new parts of the garden are outside the farmyard. An area between the farm buildings and lake has been made into a new walled garden, with a raised walk along two sides, at the corner of which Arnold Machin is constructing a summer-house and cascade over the grotto he has already completed. Along the lakeside he has made a long screen with open arches, constructed, like all the other buildings at Garmelow, with the strikingly deep-red local brick. From the new walled garden a path leads round the lake, passing the boat-house and, further on, an oriental temple designed by Francis Machin. This leads to a viewpoint facing the arched screen and, looking in another direction, to the conservatory—one of Francis Machin's earliest models—which is built against the house.

More than anything else Garmelow's individuality comes from its limited use of flowers—or any other plants—and the predominance of architectural features. At the same time the personal element is doubly important in that Arnold Machin has not only thought up and designed the buildings him-self—except the temple and conservatory—but actually constructed them as well, thereby avoiding the building costs that have made any quantity of such architectural features a rarity in gardens today.

Garmelow Manor. Francis Machin's oriental temple reflected in the lake of his father's garden.

Very different from Garmelow is the garden of Brook Cottage, Alkerton in Oxfordshire, made by Mr and Mrs David Hodges since 1964. David Hodges is an architect, but rather than making an architect's garden he has concentrated his efforts on sensitively enlarging the original house and giving it a firm unity with the new garden which flows out from it in two directions. When the Hodges came to Brook Cottage the site of their garden—four acres in size and roughly rectangular, on a fairly steep west-facing slope, with the house in one top corner—was rough grazing and cattle drank from the pond which has now been incorporated as a central feature. An important priority for the Hodges as they have steadily expanded the garden has been to blend it naturally into the fields of the surrounding countryside. Therefore areas with a hint of formality lead to more natural, open planting towards the perimeters. While in some places the ground has been levelled and banks made, in others the natural slopes have been retained and new trees and hedges have been carefully sited to create a series of winding routes through the garden.

Brook Cottage's particular charm and interest derive from its planting by Mrs Hodges, which shows adventurous variety and a keen sense of colour association. The essentially informal plan of the garden—partly dictated by the need for low maintenance so that Mr and Mrs Hodges could look after the garden themselves with the help of one gardener—means that the paths lead from areas of contrasting character and appearance. Where the garden drops away in front of the house and its entrance forecourt, down to the brook which forms the lower boundary and gives the house its name, are some of the more recent developments that reveal the Hodges' successful blending of planting and landscape. The main feature at the bottom of the slope is a serpentine lake that they have dug, David Hodges indulging his architectural leanings at one end where the lake is fed by water flowing out of a terracotta lion's head set in the stone wall of a circular raised platform. On the slope between the house and lake the garden's variety is well displayed: at one end is a new scree garden and beneath the forecourt, its planting highlighted by the clipped yew hedge behind, is a large white border. In another, south-facing, border where the colours are predominantly pink and blue are ceanothus, cistus, hibiscus, and the smaller *Convolvulus althaeoides*, with contrast provided by the bright yellow flowers of the trailing *Tropaeolum polyphyllum*.

The main part of the garden stretches along the slope from the house and the greeting is immediately impressive as one takes the narrow gateway into a paved terrace enclosed on two sides by old stone walls and on the others by yew hedges added by the Hodges. Beneath the south- and west-facing walls are borders filled with mainly tender plants: *Carpentaria californica*, *Passiflora caerulea* and *Solanum jasminoides* 'Album', for instance, and columnar cypresses have been effectively planted in old millstones, which give the terrace its name. Beyond the terrace is the garden's main lawn, reached by a wide flight of stone

Opposite Brook Cottage. Hostas and euphorbias in the foreground are among a wealth of plants around the small pond.

steps and bounded along one side by the continuing yew hedge. The arrangement of the stones on the bank along the other side is characteristic of the Hodges' ingenuity—they have been laid on black polythene which not only keeps down the weeds but is now concealed by various closely planted perennials and shrubs. The focal point at the far end of the lawn from the house is the yellow border where bright variegated foliage is matched by the hues of different flowers.

Behind the border a copper-beech hedge offsets the planting and continues on down the slope to form a tunnel with another, identical hedge. Above here the old pond is now surrounded by luxuriant bog plants; tall primulas and iris, as well as hostas, astilbes and lysichitums. Beyond the pond a tennis court is concealed in the centre of the garden and leads to the most open area stretching to the perimeters. Here shrub roses are planted individually in the grass and there are also collections of sorbus, crataegus and birch and dense plantings of viburnums—notably *Viburnum tomentosum*. Returning towards the house along the uppermost side of the garden an avenue of *Prunus* 'Shirotae' leads to where a new stone wall has been made to support various climbers behind an herbaceous border. From here one looks down into the courtyard at the back of the house, incorporated into the garden by hostas and campanulas planted between the paving stones, and clematis and roses—'Lady Hillington' is one—against the grey walls. Amongst these typical variety is added by a large *Hydrangea petiolaris* and the scarlet-flowered *Tropaeolum speciosum*.

While the Hodges have made and are continually enhancing their garden, which cleverly incorporates their house without being dominated by it, at the Old Rectory, Farnborough in Berkshire, Michael and Caroline Todhunter have created their garden on all sides of the house which was built in 1749 and forms an outstanding centrepiece. The Todhunters bought the Old Rectory in 1965. Previously it had been lived in by John Betjeman between 1945 and 1950, but although he used it as the home of Archie the bear in his delightful children's story *Archie and the Strict Baptists*, neither he nor his wife were keen gardeners.

In planning their garden the Todhunters have used the invaluable shelter provided by mature limes and beeches (no doubt planted by a thoughtful Georgian or early-Victorian parson), as the house is perched at 800 feet above sea level, overlooking the Berkshire Downs. It is probably the county's highest garden of note. The entrance front of the house looks on to lawn enclosed by beeches, but at the far end the elevated position is taken advantage of by an opening and ha-ha which, as well as concealing the road leading through the village, extends the view to Beacon Hill in the far distance.

That the Old Rectory is a garden of horticultural quality is immediately evident from the plants growing against the house, which include a white wisteria, *Clematis* 'Etoile Rose', and the Oriental *Buddleia crispa*. The house and tiled stables immediately adjoining one side form a core around which the garden unfolds in an easy progression that reveals a series of plants both unusual and perfectly suited to the house's background. Among the few main features which were inherited from predecessors were the double herbaceous borders, backed by yew hedges, to one side of the lawn in front of the house and these have been almost completely replanted by Caroline Todhunter, mainly with pastel-shaded herbaceous plants occasionally punctuated by brighter colour, for instance, the brilliant red 'Cerise Bouquet' roses.

On one side of the house is a lawn, enclosed by yew hedges and broken by an oval pool with a central statue and fountain. Facing across the lawn is a pillared summer-house, notable for the interior decoration of murals by Molly Bishop. The note of restraint in this part of the garden is the ideal introduction to the main area, behind the house, where most of Caroline Todhunter's creative efforts have been concentrated. The formality of a small courtyard decorated with lemon trees in tubs is soon ended in the rose garden, where borders of old-fashioned shrub roses, mixing with martagon lilies and euphorbias flank—and at times threaten to swamp—a central path which leads to an ideally chaste Chinese Chippendale seat. A further note of order is provided by clipped domes of *Osmarea burkwoodii* behind the borders.

Where to one side of the rose borders there was once an orchard, the apple trees (of which there is one gnarled survivor now shrouded by a 'Kiftsgate' rose) have been replaced by a variety of trees and shrubs: philadelphus for scent, a tulip tree and a ginkgo and a number of magnolias including the delicate *Magnolia wilsonii* with hanging, cup-shaped flowers. A characteristically deft touch showing a combination of practicality and decoration is the long hedge of white 'Nevada' rose which screens the orchard from the tennis court beyond.

When the Todhunters came to the Old Rectory the lower part of the garden was given over to a motley selection of vegetables. Now the boundary is marked by an immaculate beech hedge and through a wrought-iron gate a host of young plants in different beds is revealed—as well as the vegetables which have been retained and spruced up. One bed is dominated by yellow plants and has on one corner a striking *Liriodendron aureomarginatum*, the variegated tulip tree.

The boundary on one side of the garden is a mature avenue of limes and beech. The Todhunters have greatly enhanced this by opening the central view between the trees to the downs beyond and positioning a pond with numerous primulas and other aquatic plants (which do not survive in the well-drained soil in the rest of the garden) at the far end.

If most of the garden is planned to retain the traditional atmosphere of a country rectory, the trumpet call which puts the seal on the garden's individuality is the walled area around the swimming pool. Concealed from the rest of the garden by its protective walls, it is reached through white doors flanked by

'Cerise Bouquet' roses. At the far end of the pool daturas and lilies stand in tubs on either side of the part-Gothic part-Mogul summer-house which, like the surrounding walls, is cream-washed. The summer-house is open fronted to allow constant views to the downs through its huge arched window at the back. The overall effect, which is certainly most un-English, is heightened by the scented plants of mainly white, cream and yellow flowers clothing the walls: *Cytisus battandieri* and climbing roses such as 'Golden Wings', 'Paul's Lemon Pillar' and 'Alister Stellar Gray', as well as the blue of ceanothus and *Solanum crispum*. It is not only an idyllic and intoxicating place to spend a hot summer afternoon, but in addition an enviable example of how best to incorporate a swimming pool into a garden.

6
TOWARDS THE LARGER LANDSCAPE

Since the Second World War escapism, a desire for seclusion and intimacy has become a powerful motive in garden making. As a result gardens have tended to become enclosed and inward looking, their pleasures and qualities contained within fixed boundaries. This is not, however, universal. There remains unbroken the relationship between the garden and the landscape beyond which has been an important thread in the development of British gardens—at least since the beginning of the eighteenth century. During that century the relationship reached an extreme when garden and landscape were seen as one, an effortless picture of nature, simple but controlled. Since then the garden has regained its independent identity—in many different guises—and been used where possible as the foreground for a landscape, natural or man-made. While there have been few people in recent decades in a position to create a landscape—parkland or otherwise—on an eighteenth-century scale, there have been a number who have consciously created their gardens with a view to the landscape beyond. Even Hidcote, popularly regarded as the epitome of an enclosed, secret garden, was planned by Lawrence Johnston around two main vistas, progressing through the garden to vantage points affording spectacular views across the surrounding countryside.

Whether their gardens lead to parkland planted by ancestors or natural scenery, creators of such outward-looking gardens have unconsciously followed in the footsteps of one of England's more eccentric but eminently successful garden-makers, Sir George Sitwell. He wrote—in characteristically poetic language—around the turn of the century:

> It is only a part of the garden which lies within the boundary walls . . . The garden must be considered not as a thing by itself, but as a gallery of foregrounds designed to set off the soft hues of the distance; it is Nature which should call the tune, and the melody is to be found in the prospect of blue hill or shimmering lake, or mystery-haunted plain, in the aerial perspective of great trees beyond the boundary, in the green cliffs of leafy woodland which wall us in on either hand. It may be argued further that real beauty is neither in garden nor landscape, but in the relationship of both to the individual.[1]

Sir George's own garden at Renishaw Hall in Derbyshire was strongly influenced by the gardens of the Italian Renaissance he so passionately admired. It far exceeds in quality and originality any other of the 'Italian' revivalist gardens of the nineteenth and early twentieth centuries, and happily his design of yew hedges and pyramids, terraces and statues, leading to an escarpment from where the ground drops away to the lake he dug at the bottom of the hill, survives today.

Because of its geographical position Renishaw has been referred to as 'an oasis in an industrial wasteland'. It is an interesting coincidence that the description is similarly applicable to Biddick Hall in Durham, the best Italian Renaissance-inspired garden to have been made in England since the war. Biddick could be described as the dower-house for Lambton Castle, family seat of the Earls of Durham, and it stands on the edge of the large park surrounding the castle. The garden was made by Anthony Lambton who has subsequently left England to live in Italy—as did Sir George Sitwell himself after creating the garden at Renishaw.

At Biddick the garden stretches away from the west side of the house, the

Biddick. The Italian Garden, complete with columnar cypresses and terracotta urns.

ground sloping gently downwards at first, before rising at the far end and launching into the wooded parkland beyond. The long rectangular shape is enclosed by brick walls on either side and from the house there is a progression through different areas, each concealed by surrounding hedges and with only a central path leading unbroken to the distant vantage point. The essential elements are the clipped hedges—mainly beech and yew—and the beautiful urns and statues that decorate all parts of the garden.

The largest area is the wide lawn immediately in front of the house, flanked by rows of hawthorn trees, their branches clipped into square boxes supported on slender trunks. Outside the hawthorns, herbaceous borders stretch along both sides in front of the boundary walls. The lawn ends in a tall beech hedge with four stone urns in front and only the narrow central path giving a glimpse into the formal rose garden which lies immediately beyond. Within its surrounding beech hedges the rose garden is divided into four squares by yew hedges, surmounted by clipped pyramids and balls on the corners and on both sides of the entrances into each square. Each series of rose-beds centres on a *Pyrus salicifolia*, themselves clipped into neat balls of silver foliage.

Beyond the rose garden the main cross-axis of a grass walk between beech hedges, leading in one direction to the orchard and in the other to wrought-iron gates opening into the walled kitchen garden, forms the boundary with the apiary garden, where Anthony Lambton made a formal pattern in four squares, each centring on a delightful ornamental 'chinoiserie' beehive. After the apiary garden the central grass path leads between yew hedges, which form long rectangular enclosures on either side, to an open grass plateau where four stone statues of the Seasons announce the garden's theatrical finale of an enormous stone fountain enclosed by circular hedges.

The orchard to one side of the main area stretching away from the house is divided into four squares by mown grass paths. Planted with cherries and lilacs, with spring bulbs beneath, it is a refreshing contrast to the firm lines of the yew and beech hedges. The path between the rose garden and apiary garden which leads into the orchard continues through into the most recently-made area, the Italian garden, the name of which confirms the inspiration of the gardens throughout.

The Italian garden is a narrow rectangle, bordered on one side by a brick wall supporting roses and clematis, and stretching from an enclosed pool and fountain at one end, through rose gardens with fastigiate yews at the centre of square patterns of beds to a large, circular stone window from Lambton Castle, set in the ground between four standard wisteria. Beyond is a copper-beech hedge with arched openings and, the most striking feature of all, rows of tall, fastigiate cypress trees.

Biddick reveals a masterly use of contained spaces progressing to the landscape beyond, which is in the best tradition of both Italian and English garden design. The balance of influences is further revealed in the detail: on the one hand the statues and urns and the design of the Italian garden; on the other, the unmistakable Englishness of the cool beech hedges and the herbaceous borders.

At Sutton Park in Yorkshire the garden also joins the house to parkland beyond, but in a very different manner from Biddick. In place of the austere formality of clipped hedges and statuary are richly planted terraces descending from the house to a long tapestry green and copper beech hedge marking the boundary with the park beyond. Stretching to the plain of York, the park is flat, with the trees arranged in the distinctive 'Capability' Brown style. As a result the landscape has been attributed to him although there is no documentary evidence for that and it is more likely to have been the work of a later follower or admirer of Brown's style.

When Mrs Reginald Sheffield and her late husband bought Sutton Park in 1962 there was no garden to speak of other than the mature trees to either side of the main view from the south front of the house. Since then Nancy Sheffield has effectively added a third dimension to the relationship between the striking house—with its tall central block and wings and pavilions on either side, built by Thomas Atkinson between 1720 and 1740—and the park which was laid out shortly after the house had been completed. While the firm architectural lines of the terraces retain a feeling of formality in keeping with the house's classical façade, the abundant planting in borders both softens the lines and enhances the overall picture to a significant degree. The key to the terraces' overall success is the fact that their dimensions and the planting are on a sufficiently bold scale not to be overshadowed by the house on one side or the park beyond.

The uppermost terrace immediately in front of the house is paved, with squares of lawn, and planting is limited to climbers and wall-plants against the house and a mixed border, containing shrub roses and standard wisteria underplanted with tulips and, later, euphorbias, along the retaining wall. This is broken by a generously wide flight of stone steps leading down to the middle terrace where the most concentrated planting is to be found. This terrace was originally designed by Percy Cane, late in his career, as what must have been a rather dull, formal hybrid-tea rose garden reminiscent of numerous country-house gardens between the wars. Fortunately the roses did not like the conditions and they have now been replaced with mixed beds, retaining the same rectangular pattern, but with a considerably more varied and vigorous appearance through the year. Each of the four corner beds is dominated by a clipped *Pyrus salicifolia*, and in all of them tulips, iris and hostas are followed by summer-flowering perennials, shrubs and standard roses.

In addition to this pattern of beds, Mrs Sheffield has made a deep mixed border beneath the upper retaining wall which is now virtually hidden by the dense planting. *Viburnum carlesii*, lilacs, philadelphus and Judas trees,

94

One of the Italian classical statues which adorn the garden at Biddick.

Sutton Park. The view across the terraces to the house, revealing the degree of harmony between architecture and planting.

Sutton Park. Looking across the formal pool on the lowest terrace to a fine cedar with, on the right, the beech hedge which forms the boundary with the park.

arranged symmetrically on either side of the central steps, provide a framework for lower shrubs, foliage plants and herbaceous plants such as blocks of delphiniums. At either end bronze female statues stand on tall brick pedestals in front of ornamental white metal arbours on the upper terrace, each shrouded by *Clematis montana*.

Architectural formality returns on the third and lower terrace where a wide expanse of lawn is broken only by a lily canal. The canal's rectangular shape extends on one side into a semicircle, matching the line of the boundary beech hedge which forms a central bow and is filled by a semicircular stone seat. From across the terraces the house's strong vertical elevations are repeated by a line of tall columnar cypresses along the bottom retaining wall and another pair on either side of the upper flight of central steps.

The tapestry beech hedge forms an unbroken boundary with the park beyond, but on the bottom terrace the lawn stretches out on either side and leads eventually to woodland walks extending along both sides of the park. Here ornamental trees, particularly flowering cherries, have been added to the native varieties and underplanted with daffodils which have naturalized into huge drifts. In one direction the walk leads to a temple and eventually the walks cross the open parkland to meet in the centre, opposite the house.

The garden's most important architectural feature is the new orangery Mrs Sheffield has built against the house, at the east end of the upper terrace. It was designed by Francis Johnson, the leading classical architect in the north-east,

Abbots Ripton. The double herbaceous border with the trelliswork rondel designed by Peter Foster in the background.

Ince Castle. The majestic view across the Lynher River.

who is based in York, and who has made a number of alterations to the interior of the house.

Sutton Park is an outstanding example of how a recently added garden can not only complete but considerably enhance an existing picture of house and park, in a manner that was rarely achieved before the war. The terraces themselves show the adventurous planting within the confines of an orderly plan which is such a decisive characteristic of good post-war gardens.

Since the late 1950s, at Abbots Ripton Hall in Cambridgeshire, Lord de Ramsey has created what he himself calls 'pleasure grounds and ornamental gardens'[2] extending to twenty acres around his home. For the majority of gardeners today 'pleasure grounds' is a phrase from the eighteenth century at the latest, and it conjures up pictures of ladies perambulating along serpentine paths in ankle-length dresses, being pursued by ardent suitors, and certainly very few people consciously think of their gardens as ornamental. Such an apparently old-fashioned description would seem to point to something rather different, which is in many ways what Abbots Ripton is.

In the creation of his garden Lord de Ramsey has been assisted at different times by Humphrey Waterfield and Lanning Roper with the lay-out and

Abbots Ripton Hall. The view down the double herbaceous borders with, in the foreground, the Gothic trelliswork rondel designed by Peter Foster.

Opposite Hazelby House. The gates into the kitchen garden with double borders beyond.

planting, and by the architect Peter Foster who designed the buildings and other ornaments which add so decisively to the garden's appearance. The overall plan and initial ideas have, however, been Lord de Ramsey's. His great success has been to retain the established qualities of the site, notably the outstanding mature trees, and not only enrich them with a number of new features, but also give the garden a bold design that radiates from the house into the flat but rich farmland beyond, once part of Huntingdonshire. The garden's most important natural feature is the Abbots Ripton brook, which runs in on one side and winds its way through the garden. The first sign of the various striking architectural features is given from the small lane leading up to the house, by a white Moorish screen designed by Peter Foster.

Where the brook first enters the garden it is crossed by a small footbridge, with Doric columns and a grotto against the boundary wall behind, and its passage is formalized into a rectangular canal along the edge of the lawn sloping down from the house. In the centre of the canal is a simple jet fountain and on the far side from the house tall yew hedges screen what lies beyond with only an opening opposite the fountain. Through here Lord de Ramsey has created the garden's most important vista, leading right to the boundary with the farmland beyond, whose formality is quite different from the more wandering path outwards which is taken in another direction by following the course of the brook. A central grass path is flanked by herbaceous borders as it leads gently uphill for a hundred yards to white wrought-iron gates beyond which a chestnut avenue continues the view into the surrounding countryside.

With paving flags along their edges—to enable plants to spread forward naturally, thereby breaking the regimental lines without upsetting the mower —the borders are planted for the late summer and early autumn, and filled almost exclusively with herbaceous perennials enhanced in places by annuals to add brighter colour. They are backed by alternating yew and golden philadelphus, both clipped into formal drum shapes. At some distance up the central path from the canal is a pair of stone cherubs and, beyond this, the borders are broken by the far more striking and important rondel of wooden trellis-work, designed by Peter Foster, whose curving screens are surmounted by Gothic finials. If unexpected, the rondel is none the less perfectly suited to the borders' considerable scale while the slender finials give a marvellous vertical element to the plants as one approaches up the central path.

To one side, beyond the remnants of an orchard where the old apple and pear trees are now filled with climbing roses and clematis, a cupressus hedge conceals another long border filled with grey and silver foliage plants which thrive in the south-facing position against the boundary wall. The careful arrangement of plants gives constant variety of shape with low artemesia, helichrysum, lavender and many herbs in front and tall buddleias, abutilons and pollarded eucalyptus behind. At the top of the border is an area of further variety, with a wall covered with small-flowered clematis and a path crossed by rose arches between rows of vegetables.

What was another area of orchard, on the far side of the main borders, is now planted with mixed ornamental trees, notably acers, sorbus and magnolias. Between here and the brook is the iris garden, where formally arranged beds have been planted around a central statue of a female figure. Nearby the brook is crossed by a white-painted wooden bridge in a Chinese Chippendale pattern.

Beyond the bridge the lawn, which slopes from the house to the canal and fountain, sweeps round and opens out on the south-east side of the house, where the original Regency architecture is displayed without trace of the Victorian alterations by Anthony Salvin evident elsewhere. On this side the white columns of the bowed portico face across the lawn to a vista between white borders, highlighted in summer by the rose 'Blanc Double de Coubert' on either side, which lead into shrubberies and a more varied progress through the garden towards the landscape beyond.

At one point along the white borders an opening turns into the circular rose garden, where old-fashioned shrub roses have been planted around a circular lawn. The roses are backed by large shrubs, including many sea-buckthorns, and beyond grass paths wind around a number of informally planted specimens —such as *Koelreuteria paniculata* and *Robinia frisia*. From the red-brick, three-arched eighteenth-century bridge on the edge of the garden, which closes the vista along the white borders, the brook winds its way back, beneath another wooden bridge, past an octagonal, thatched summer-house with Gothic windows designed by Peter Foster and beneath some of the enormous elms— which having survived the epidemic disease are the most interesting and unusual of the garden's mature trees—to the white Chippendale bridge. Between its bank on one side and densely planted island beds of shrubs are two young trees that reveal the discerning eye that Lord de Ramsey has brought to bear on the garden—*Taxodium ascendans*, a columnar Swamp Cypress, and *Catalpa x erubescens* 'Purpurea', a purple-leafed catalpa.

Close to the eighteenth-century, red-brick bridge Lord de Ramsey's gratitude to Humphrey Waterfield is shown by an urn erected shortly after the latter's death and inscribed, 'Remember Humphrey Waterfield who made this garden anew. Nov. 1971'. It is beyond here that the garden enjoys its most successful and surprising fusion with the landscape beyond, as one looks out across the placid water of a five-acre lake. The scene might be more commonplace if, as one would expect, the lake had been dug during the eighteenth or nineteenth centuries. In fact, it was dug in 1970, essentially to provide a reservoir for Lord de Ramsey's farming irrigation system, while on the far side a bank has been raised and planted with groups of poplars to deaden the noise from the main road beyond. The outward prospect across the lake from the edge of the garden

The thatched summer-house at Abbots Ripton, designed by Peter Foster.

Ince Castle. The view from the swimming pool on a sheltered terrace to the wide sweep of the Lynher River and the landscape beyond.

is given a focal point by the Chinese fishing pavilion, again designed by Peter Foster, which Lord de Ramsey has positioned as an eye-catcher on the far bank. (Although declared Chinese, the design of the pavilion is taken from a building in a watercolour by Constable which hangs in Abbots Ripton.) Certainly the creation of a landscape feature such as the lake for both utilitarian and decorative purposes is something of which all the best eighteenth-century landscapists—practical men, as well as artistic—would have heartily approved.

There was no need for the creation of landscape features at Ince Castle, near Saltash in Cornwall, when the late Viscount Boyd of Merton and his wife bought the castle in 1960. This delightful and highly individual building looks—from the outside—both castle and house. It is square and unusually constructed of grey and red brick rather than the predominantly used local stone and its main façades are battlemented between squat corner towers. The building stands on a promontory which is almost made an island by the River Lynher sweeping round in a long curve. From its elevated position Ince commands spectacular views, to the south, south-east and south-west, across the water to Devon on the far side.

Ince's initial appeal for Lord and Lady Boyd was largely its isolated position, making it a viable retreat from his busy public life, and offering him the opportunity to indulge his love of sailing. It was only after the necessary restoration to the house had been carried out that they turned their attention to the garden and set about creating something which had its own individuality as well as providing a foreground for the landscape beyond.

What little garden the Boyds had inherited was to the south of the castle. Retaining nothing except old walls on both sides, which they considerably rebuilt and extended, they laid out a series of large terraces that dropped away gently from the house. The first, paved terrace leads to lawn and both of these are flanked by raised beds filled with mixed shrubs—many of them tender and benefiting from Ince's mild, if windswept, conditions. Stone steps lead from the lawn to the lowest terrace where a formal pattern of beds is divided by brick and cobble paths at right angles which meet at a central sundial. The planting in the beds is again mixed; shrub roses, *Magnolia stellata*, and different dwarf rhododendrons, such as the white 'Cowslip' and yellow 'Reo', as well as tender leptospernum, correas and unusual salvias. Beyond this formal garden is a rectangular canal pool running across the terrace and a semicircular stone seat recessed into the lower wall.

At each end of the canal pool are two of the garden's many unusual figures—here stone cherubs riding snails—most of which came from the courtyard of Lady Boyd's father, the second Earl of Iveagh's house in St James's Square in London.[3] The canal's position at right angles to the terraces leads off naturally in both directions, one way past a small octagonal gazebo and the

101

other through an opening in the wall to a wide lawn which now sweeps up past the east front of the house. The lawn was made by extensive levelling and by taking in a field. It leads to a new ha-ha beyond which the ground drops away to the river, with Antony House on the far side, its elegant grey façade just visible through the trees of its park and gardens. A long, curving shrub border has been made along the wall which forms the boundary with the terraces to the south of the house and, on the outward edge of the lawn, are large island beds with photinias and amalanchiers, which have been judiciously positioned to provide interest without obscuring the view.

From the north-east corner of the lawn a cherry walk leads off into what was originally overgrown woodland. This has been steadily cleared and planted to make a woodland garden of marked contrast to the areas to the south and east of the house. Benefiting from the shelter of the tall trees are camellias, magnolias and rhododendrons, and more tender *Stachyurus praecox* and *Azara lanceolata*. While most of Ince is not at all typical of Cornish gardens, renowned for their displays of exotic Asiatic trees and shrubs, here in the woodland garden are many plants with names recalling famous Cornish gardens such as the rhododendrons 'Alison Johnstone' from Trewithen and 'Caerhays Lawrence' from Caerhays Castle. The woodland opens out in the centre into a clear glade with naturalized cowslips and, to one side, a cascade where abundant water—rare in this garden whose thin topsoil lies over quick-draining shale—supports primulas and other aquatic plants. Another path leads out of the woodland and back to the west (entrance) front of the house, passing the most striking legacy from the past, an enormous Turkey oak blown down over fifty years ago but still happily alive in its recumbent position.

To the south-west of the house Lady Boyd has taken advantage of existing walls to make an enclosed white garden. Nearby new walls now shelter a summer garden whose central area is paved. On all sides are deep borders filled with shrubs and perennials with red, orange or yellow flowers or foliage; a copper pittisporum, roses 'Charles Austin' and, over a metal bower at one end, 'School Girl', a pink *Acer palmatum*, *Cytisus battandieri* and azaras. With its bright 'hot' colours, this garden comes into its own in the late summer and carries on from the flowering in the white garden and the formal beds on the south terraces.

The most impressive views over the river estuary and gentle hills beyond are to be gained from the lowest terrace to the south-west of the house where the Boyds have made a swimming pool. It is from here that the full benefit of creating a garden in such an enviable natural position is brought home, as well as the manner in which the garden has been planned to make full use of the advantages offered.

When Martin Lane Fox, a brother of Robin who is well known for his gardening books and column in the *Financial Times*, bought Hazelby House

Hazelby House. The formal canal and temple which form a cross-axis to the double borders running down to the lake.

Ince Castle. Looking through a gateway across the formal pool at the bottom of the terraces to the octagonal 'shellhouse'.

near Newbury in 1974, his first action was to remove the top, third storey which had been added to the early-Victorian house around the turn of this century. This made the house more manageable and replaced an ugly, gabled skyline with a more elegant flat-roofed, balustraded one. A year later, when he turned his attention to creating a garden his attitude was equally decisive and in ten years the series of enclosures and impressive vistas have acquired exceptional maturity and harmony with the surrounding countryside.

When he began, the site had few existing qualities. To the north-west of the house the walled kitchen garden was overgrown and to the west—now the main garden area—the terrain was extremely uneven. This was transformed with the help of a bulldozer into a series of levels, with retaining brick walls and interlinking flights of stone or brick steps. To the south the ground now slopes gently away to a lake sheltered by tall trees and to the west of the slope the garden flows easily into the fields beyond. The keynote of the garden's design is the balance between the series of intimate symmetrical compartments, enclosed by clipped hedges, and the bold relationship of the garden with its surroundings. In all areas the garden is richly clothed with planting that, like the design, has been devised by Martin Lane Fox himself.

The ambitious note to be found throughout the gardens is first sounded by a double axis stretching away to the west of the house. A wide grass path flanked by thuja and holly hedges runs adjacent to double borders leading to a lead statue. The shrubs which predominate in the borders are divided at intervals by bays of alternating brick and stone paving which contain, on one side, stone urns and on the other lead figures of a shepherd and shepherdess. The simple

Hazelby House. The lily pool and contemplative bust enclosed by yew hedges.

grass path passes the entrance to the old walled garden, the dramatically revamped appearance of which is heralded by white wooden gates forming a Gothic arch at the entrance. From the gates double herbaceous borders on each side of a gravel path extend right across the garden, backed by beech hedges and highlighted in late summer by standard buddleias on both sides. A white wooden, trellis-work arbour covered in 'New Dawn' roses gives the borders an ideal architectural centrepiece and from here paths extend at right angles to a sheltered swimming pool garden on one side and between immaculate rectangles of vegetables on the other to a stone statue on the far side of the garden. Tucked into a corner of the walled garden is a small, secret, white garden. The popularity of Vita Sackville-West's original at Sissinghurst may have made white gardens almost obligatory in any fashion-conscious garden of recent decades, but few are as successful as Hazelby's where roses clamber up trellis-work pillars and, below, smaller plants flow out of the formally arranged beds over brick paths which lead to a central sundial.

Immediately to the west of the house what was a paved terrace has been partly covered by a new orangery, strengthening the link of house to garden and containing automatic blinds and ventilation which would have astounded that genius of Victorian glasshouses, Joseph Paxton. Steps from the terrace lead up to what was one of the first enclosures to be made, the old-fashioned rose garden where that sought-after state of ordered profusion has been successfully achieved. Enclosed by yew hedges, the garden is divided by brick paths. Wooden arbours support climbing roses while in the borders contained by clipped box hedges, shrub roses are thickly underplanted with herbaceous plants.

On the far side of the rose garden from the house the mood changes immediately as a flight of steps leads up into a larger rectangular compartment, again enclosed by yew hedges and containing lawn surrounding a long formal lily pool with a sombre bust at the far end. Until this enclosure was made there was a simple lawn, for cricket for junior Lane Foxes, with a white bench at the far end. The lily pool has retained that basic simplicity but at the same time has added strong architectural interest to this part of the garden.

In contrast to the closed vistas here and at the end of the main double shrub borders, the large area of garden to the south-west of the house—the most recent to be developed—looks expansively outwards. From the lawn below the retaining wall of the rose garden there extends a wide grass path down the southward slope between wide borders backed by rows of sorbus, to the distant focal point of the rotunda which Martin Lane Fox has positioned on an island in the lake. Halfway down the slope the borders are divided by an equally impressive cross-axis. A classical temple, built by the Derbyshire firm of Haddonstone and complete with Tuscan columns and portico, looks along a rectangular canal with raised stone edges, and forms a le Nôtre-style *patte d'oie*

Hazelby House. The rose arbour covered with 'New Dawn' which forms the centrepiece of the borders in the old walled garden.

Nantclwyd. The house rebuilt for the late Sir Vivyan Naylor-Leyland by Clough Williams-Ellis, who also redesigned the gardens. Here the formal garden stretches away from one side of the house.

for three vistas which cut through hedges to the parkland beyond. When the hedges have grown to maturity the perspective of the vistas will be considerably increased and it is not too fanciful to imagine that the picture will recall the stately *allées* in the famous garden of Martin Lane Fox's family home, Bramham Park in Yorkshire. Certainly Hazelby is a contemporary garden which combines to an unusual degree historical and horticultural inspiration from different sources with a vigorous individuality.

Sir Clough Williams-Ellis was responsible for two unusual gardens, unusual because they were laid out around new country houses and devised to link the houses with superb established parkland settings. Clough Williams-Ellis was born into a Welsh landowning family and his off-beat and at times flamboyant career as an architect earned him a mixed reputation. Much of his time was spent rebuilding or altering houses for friends and acquaintances and his best-known work remains the eccentric, decorative village of Portmeirion in North Wales, mainly created between the wars. He was almost wholly interested in working on houses and, as he once remarked, 'I have never built a block of flats, or offices, or a shop, or a factory, or a cinema anywhere—nor wanted to.'[4] He had already shown his penchant for planning garden features both at Portmeirion and his own North Wales home, Plas Brondanw, which he rebuilt after a fire in 1951, when he received probably the most ambitious commission of his career—to rebuild Nantclwyd Hall, in North Wales also, for Sir Vivyan Naylor-Leyland.

Sir Vivyan originally wanted to move from his enormous house at Nantclwyd to another site on the estate, but Clough was able to persuade him to stay put. He demolished and rebuilt much of the house, cleared away all of the unhappy hotch-potch of buildings to one side, except the stables, and enhanced the landscape of the park. This was all executed to Clough's designs with notable success. To the south of the house, in place of the demolished buildings he made the main new garden, with a broad paved terrace along the house leading to a formal, walled rectangle with yew buttresses along the walls and two pairs of pavilions on either side. Through ornamental wrought-iron gates at the far end he erected the dramatic eye-catcher of a tall stone obelisk. In the larger parkland setting on the other sides of the house he built two ornamental bridges across the river for the new drive and positioned a collection of somewhat extraordinary animal statuary at different points, including a grotesque seated boar who gazes towards the house from a grassy eminence to one side. The most successful of Clough's additions to the landscape was the octagonal, domed rotunda which he erected in a roundel of trees on a knoll at one end of the large lake, ideally positioned to enhance the view from the house along the spectacular wooded valley which stretches into the distance beyond. The whole project was theatrical to a degree and greatly appealed to the architect.

The rotunda in the park at Nantclwyd,
a flourish of landscape design by
Clough Williams-Ellis.

Dalton Hall. The garden front of the house built by Clough Williams-Ellis for the
Mason-Hornbys in the late 1960s with, in the background, the temple Williams-Ellis
designed using the four columns of the old house's portico.

On a less flamboyant scale than Nantclwyd was Williams-Ellis's work at Dalton Hall, in Westmorland. It was his last house, which he began in 1968, when he was aged eighty. Whereas at Nantclwyd he had advised and carried out partial demolition and rebuilding at Dalton he decided this was not practical and suggested a completely new house. Once his clients, Mr and Mrs Anthony Mason-Hornby, who had recently inherited Dalton and its estate, had agreed, the project was begun. In many ways Dalton is perhaps Clough Williams-Ellis's most satisfactory house, an elegant Georgian rectangle covered in pink-washed stucco, with a hipped roof of Westmorland slates, sash windows and, on its two main fronts, pediments and Tuscan pilasters. It replaced a building which was riddled with dry rot and impossible to run without an army of servants, with a home of quality and authority that could be managed with no resident staff.

Integral to Clough's designs for Dalton were his plans for the garden which involved integrating the house into the undulating parkland that surrounds it. Between the entrance front and the charming old stable building he laid out a forecourt with cobbled bricks, enclosing a circular paved sweep for cars around a central lawn and fountain. On either side rows of pleached limes were planted in front of low stone walls that in places follow the external lines of the older, much larger house. At strategic points specially designed new wrought-iron gates set in tall stone piers elegantly lead out of the forecourt into the garden.

His treatment of the garden front was equally successful. Along the house he laid out a broad paved terrace and beyond, slightly sunken, an area of horseshoe-shaped garden, enclosed by hornbeam hedges which terminate in an impressive pair of stone gate piers surmounted by eagles. As one looks from the house, the wide central grass path leading to the piers is flanked by columnar Irish yews behind which are crescent-shaped beds of closely planted shrubs. While the hedges give necessary protection from wind they are low enough not to obscure views out into the park. The terrace is divided from the garden beyond by a broad gravelled path stretching between an urn of impressive size at one end—a legacy from the old garden—to a new temple Clough built on top of a grass rise on the far side of the garden. The temple has a copper dome and is open-fronted, its four columns were taken from the portico of the old house. The lawns and older area of garden, dating from the original house, stretch away from the temple at right angles to the gravel walk along one side of the house and forecourt. Considering that before the war there were twelve gardeners at Dalton—five of them, admittedly, working full time in the ranges of greenhouses now demolished—and that the new garden is now maintained by the Mason-Hornbys themselves with occasional help with heavy work from one man working on the estate, the rationalization of the garden has been as successful as it has been in the house. At the same time the atmosphere of a country house set in its own parkland has been retained—if anything, enhanced by the new garden designs. No wonder that the architect recorded characteristically on completing the job when he was ninety: 'It is very warming to have ended my long building career with so satisfactory a last fling.'[5]

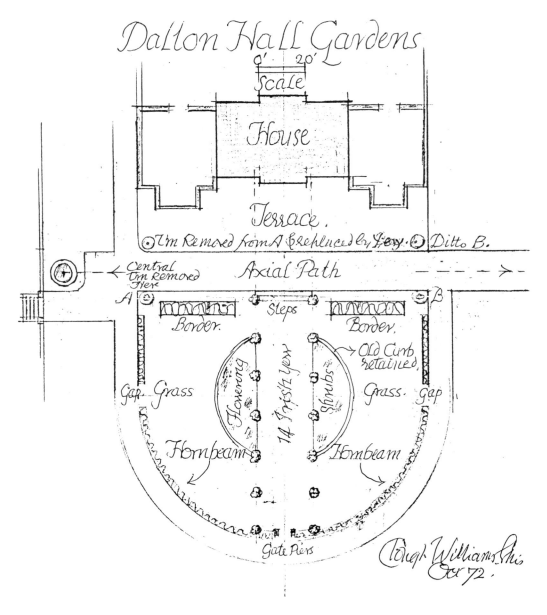

Clough Williams-Ellis's plan for the garden at Dalton Hall.

7

THE ENCHANTED WOODLAND

In *The English Garden*, published in 1964, Edward Hyams argues that Britain's outstanding gardens are divided into three categories. There are those historical gardens created at different times in the past and preserved—as far as possible—in their original form, and gardens which are, broadly speaking, in the Hidcote mould. The third category he describes as

> . . . the woodland gardens, in some ways the most romantic, the nearest to the 'paradise' of the English dream, gardens in which plants, for the most part shrubs, of the most gorgeous and exotic beauty, are so set as to simulate a 'natural' woodland scene, although in nature no such plants are found growing all together. Such gardens are the product of two influences, that of the great plantsmen and plant-collectors; and that of Robinson's *The Wild Garden*.[1]

For over a century such woodland gardens have provided ideal settings for many of the trees and shrubs introduced from overseas. They have been particularly successful in the south-west of England, Wales and the west coast of Scotland, which offer these plants a highly suitable mild and damp climatic habitat. During the nineteenth and early twentieth centuries a number of gardens were made on a huge scale, with large acreages of woodland being surrounded by protecting shelter-belts of trees and systematically thinned and replanted with exotic flowering specimens. Three of the best known of these are Inverewe in north-west Scotland, Caerhays Castle in Cornwall and Bodnant in North Wales. Very often the creators of such gardens were men who either initiated or provided the necessary funds for the expeditions of plant-collectors which brought back the first seeds or plants that were to revolutionize the character and appearance of British gardens.

If the flow of new varieties into Britain has virtually ceased since the Second World War—not only have many of the most fruitful areas such as south-west China become politically inaccessible, but the quantity of plants now readily available has minimized demand for new introductions—the significance of the type of garden to which they gave birth has, if anything, greatly increased. At a time when gardens demanding a continuous high labour input have become expensive luxuries, the informal, low-maintenance style of the woodland garden has become widely appealing. As Sylvia Crowe wrote: 'The woodland garden is labour-saving because the trees keep down the growth of rank weeds and coarse grass, and the selected plants can easily be kept clean, growing either straight out of the leaf-mould of the forest floor or from a carpet of easily managed woodland grass or low woodland plants.'[2]

Partly because of its climate and terrain the west coast of Scotland has attracted a number of outstanding gardeners and become as renowned as any region of Britain for its woodland gardens. Some of these men have been true horticultural pioneers, not least Osgood Mackenzie, who in the 1860s enclosed, with shelter-belts of conifers, sixty of the most remote acres in Britain on the west coast of Ross-shire and set about creating his garden of Inverewe. Since then a number of gardens that were begun before the Second World War have been steadily built up and expanded. At Crarae Lodge, in Argyll, Sir Ilay Campbell has considerably enhanced the garden begun by his grandparents and expanded by his father, while at nearby Strone House the late Lord Glenkinglas, from 1947 until his death in 1984, steadily built up a collection of rhododendrons in a woodland setting provided by spectacularly tall conifers, planted during the late nineteenth century.

Even compared to any of his adventurous forerunners on the west coast, one of the most intrepid gardeners to have come to the area must be Colonel Sir James Horlick. For many years Sir James had been gardening in Berkshire, principally growing rhododendrons when, in 1944, he bought the tiny and remote island of Gigha with a view to establishing a new garden somewhere more sympathetic to tender plants. Gigha is barely sixteen square miles in size and lies off the Mull of Kintyre. The presence of Islay further out to sea does little to alleviate the constant battering by Atlantic winds to which Gigha is subjected. Having restored Achamore House—the only house of any substance on the island—Sir James moved to Gigha after the Second World War and from then until a few years before his death in 1972 devoted himself to the creation of a garden around his new home. Sir James left his plant collection to the National Trust for Scotland who, together with David Landale who bought Gigha after Sir James's death, have maintained the gardens.

The background for Sir James's garden was fifty acres of woodland planted by a previous owner of Gigha to give Achamore House some shelter from the incessant wind. Sir James began by slowly clearing paths and making open glades amongst the trees and moving peat from a nearby ridge with wheelbarrows and a horse and cart since there were no tractors on the island. Using existing features such as ponds, and the bank stretching along one side of the garden behind the house, the garden developed steadily around a series of main paths running roughly parallel through the woodland, with smaller paths leading off into areas of continually varied appearance. To afford further shelter much of the woodland was divided by hedges: of escallonia, elaeagnus and

112

Ince Castle. The formal beds divided by brick and cobble paths
around a sundial on one of the lower terraces on one side of the house.

Achamore House, Gigha. The flowers of the rare and tender-scented *Rhododendron burmanicum*.

Knightshayes. Looking from the formal gardens towards the Garden in the Wood.

Great Comp. A view along one of the garden's more formal paths
to the focal point of 'Pope's Urn'.

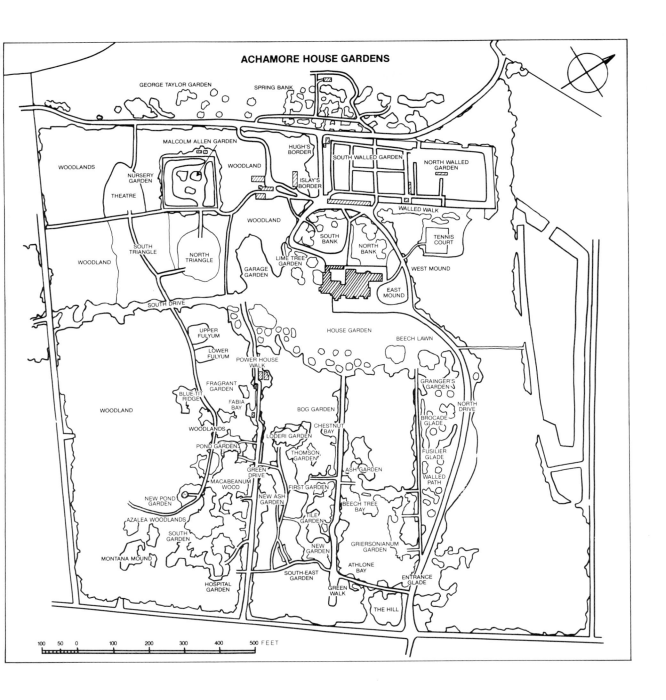

ACHAMORE HOUSE GARDENS

GEORGE TAYLOR GARDEN
SPRING BANK

MALCOLM ALLEN GARDEN
HUGH'S BORDER
SOUTH WALLED GARDEN
NORTH WALLED GARDEN

WOODLANDS
WOODLAND
ISLAY'S BORDER

NURSERY GARDEN
THEATRE
WOODLAND
WALLED WALK

SOUTH TRIANGLE
NORTH TRIANGLE
WOODLAND
SOUTH BANK
NORTH BANK
TENNIS COURT

WOODLAND
GARAGE GARDEN
LIME TREE GARDEN
WEST MOUND

SOUTH DRIVE
EAST MOUND

UPPER FULYUM
HOUSE GARDEN
BEECH LAWN

LOWER FULYUM
POWER HOUSE WALK
GRAINGER'S GARDEN
NORTH DRIVE

FRAGRANT GARDEN
BLUE-TIT RIDGE
FABIA BAY
BOG GARDEN
BROCADE GLADE

WOODLAND
WOODLANDS
CHESTNUT BAY
FUSILIER GLADE

POND GARDEN
LODERI GARDEN
THOMSON GARDEN
WALLED PATH

GREEN DRIVE
ASH GARDEN

MACABEANUM WOOD
FIRST GARDEN

NEW POND GARDEN
NEW ASH GARDEN
BEECH TREE BAY

AZALEA WOODLANDS
TILE GARDEN

SOUTH GARDEN
GRIERSONIANUM GARDEN

MONTANA MOUND
NEW GARDEN
ATHLONE BAY
ENTRANCE GLADE

HOSPITAL GARDEN
SOUTH-EAST GARDEN
GREEN WALK

THE HILL

100 50 0   100   200   300   400   500 FEET

griselinia which gave the gardens a greater feeling of secrecy. Because of their uninhibited growth many of the hedges have had to be severely pruned in recent years and this has opened up many parts of the garden for new planting.

Most of the garden is within the woodland, but in his planning of the long theatrical drive, originally hemmed in by dense ponticum rhododendrons, Sir James revealed that he was as much artist as plantsman. Having cleared the ponticums, he planted deciduous azaleas in great clumps, with open grass spaces around them, on either side of the drive. Towards the top of the drive hedges of the tender New Zealand plant *Olearia paniculata* now form tall screens behind the azaleas, while an exotic note is added by equally tender *Cordyline Australis*.

Rhododendrons were always Sir James's gardening passion and, as one might expect, they predominate in the woodland garden, certain areas being devoted to certain types. Some, such as the small, violet-flowered 'Songbird' are hybrids which Sir James raised himself. The Spring Bank is planted with early-flowering varieties, and, most notably, a selection of tender rhododendrons such as *Rh. burmanicum* and *Rh. polyandrum* that are an almost uniquely rare sight. Elsewhere is the Macabeanum Wood, planted with large-leafed varieties and in most of the open glades rhododendrons and azaleas of innumerable varieties mix with other plants.

The extreme remoteness of the garden on Gigha adds, of course, to its character and its romantic appeal. Certainly the garden reveals that, given protection from the wind, the island's mild and wet maritime climate is ideally suited to many tender trees and shrubs which are rarely seen in gardens elsewhere in Britain. As well as these, Asiatic primulas, mecanopses, gunnera and lysichitums thrive in the many boggy parts of the wood. As Edward Hyams wrote of the garden, 'The best way to see this garden is to wander slowly, alone, and preferably lost, for several days from glade to glade.'[3]

The creation of the woodland garden at Knightshayes, near Tiverton in Devon, by the late Sir John and Lady Heathcoat-Amory would be a source of considerable encouragement to any novice gardener if he or she knew that the Amorys possessed extremely limited knowledge and experience when they started. Since Sir John's death the garden has become a property of the National Trust who now maintain it jointly with Lady Amory. The Amorys came to live at Knightshayes in 1937, but work on the garden did not begin in earnest until after the war.

The imposing house, built by William Burges in the 1870s overlooks Victorian terraces and parkland sloping away downhill to the River Exe. The Amorys' first tentative steps were to simplify the over-fussy design and planting of the terraces; but it was only when this was complete that they determined to embark on creating a completely different kind of garden in the large area of woodland on one side of the terraces. The Amorys were given invaluable

Achamore House, Gigha. Hostas, gunnera, primulas and other damp-loving plants in the woodland garden.

advice in the early years by Sir Eric Savill, whose initial conception and master-minding of the Savill and Valley gardens in Windsor Great Park has been one of the finest achievements of this century.

The Garden in the Wood at Knightshayes, as it has always been known, expanded steadily as small areas of woodland were taken in, the undergrowth cleared and tall beech, chestnut and oaks thinned out to let in light and allow space for new specimens. From the original Garden in the Wood the planting has been extended more recently into new areas: Holly's Wood, Sir John's Wood, and Michael's Wood, the latter named after Michael Hickson who became head gardener in 1963 and now runs the gardens for the National Trust. The total area is over twenty acres.

Such a large area has enabled the planning to take place on a generous scale so that throughout the garden there is a feeling of space, the paths leading from one wide glade to another between areas of constantly varied planting. As well as the size of the overall area, the garden's outstanding feature is the variety of plants both in terms of type and size. Where old trees have been removed more unusual ones have now grown up to take their place: a great many magnolias, including some of the largest varieties such as *Magnolia campbellii*, nothofagus—the South American beech—and many unusual pines and other conifers, all originating from different parts of the world. In contrast to these trees are the smallest of woodland flowers which abound: primroses and primulas, cyclamen, hellebores, fritillaries and, perhaps best of all, quantities of yellow,

115

Great Comp. Steps leading up to a stone balustrade on one side of the house from where paths lead off into the woodland area of the garden.

pink and white erythroniums. In many places these plants are enclosed by peat walls which give protection and add a note of order without disturbing the overall informality.

The Amorys always hoped that their woodland garden would retain colour and interest through much of the year and their success is pointed to by the variety of shrubs. Although planted in great quantities, rhododendrons, azaleas and camellias do not submerge, in the way they are prone to do, the other shrubs, and at different times of the year euonymus, cornus, philadelphus and many other more unusual species come into their own. It is, however, in the overall balance of trees, shrubs and smaller plants that the essence of Knightshayes' quality lies. This, and the way the garden demonstrates how a woodland setting can be steadily adapted over a number of years, largely account for the widespread reputation the garden has achieved and retained.

Unlike Knightshayes—or Achamore House for that matter—there was no natural woodland setting at Great Comp in Kent when Mr and Mrs Cameron

116

embarked, in the late 1950s, on creating a new garden—partly on an old garden site and partly on open market-garden ground. The Camerons' main aspiration was to use a wide variety of trees and shrubs, planted to give an informal appearance and enable them to maintain the four and a half acres themselves. Since then the area has expanded to seven acres, and the garden that has emerged is intrinsically modern in that its priorities are to combine the particular qualities of individual plants with their association in groups as well as low maintenance. By no means all of the garden can be described as woodland. There are also formal lawns, borders and paved walks around the house and a number of architectural features added by the Camerons, such as the ruins, but the overall pattern of the main area is natural and informal, with paths leading between intensely planted trees and shrubs of seemingly limitless quantity. There are over 3,000 different plants in the garden, and larger varieties are closely underplanted with smaller evergreens, heathers and herbaceous perennials.

The woodland atmosphere was initially encouraged by quick-growing pines, larch, birch and spruce planted in some places as shelter-belts and in others to outline glades and vistas, but essentially its character has developed as the trees and shrubs themselves have grown to maturity and filled out the areas between the skeleton of paths. Now the planting in many areas is dense, like *maquis*, enabling the progression of paths gradually to unravel the garden piece by piece.

The main area of woodland walks and planting form the east and south sides of the garden, the shape of which is essentially rectangular and extends in the south-west corner to where a temple, built in 1975, marks the focal point at the end of the long path along the garden's southern boundary. The garden's main vista stretches from this side up to the house and across lawn where the curving edges are flanked by the towering bodies of different evergreens, underplanted with heathers. The extensive use of conifers and evergreens has played a vital role in shaping the garden's appearance.

Towards the south-west corner of the garden is a small glade where the aspect is more open than in other areas, yet the quantity and diversity of plants is characteristically extensive. Among the larger trees is a selection of unusual pines and a nearby cedar; there is a group of mixed magnolias, different viburnum, cornus and azaleas, a *Halesia carolina*, one of the most delicate of flowering trees, while dense ground-cover is provided by hardy geraniums, lamiums, hostas, hellebores, polygonum, euphorbias and sedum. Like many woodland gardens, Great Comp is a place that repays exploration, for it is the individual interest of its myriad contents and their associations, rather than the overall picture, that is of primary importance.

At Broadleas, near Devizes in Wiltshire, Lady Anne Cowdray found a natural site well suited to the woodland garden she has created. At the same time, although winter frosts can often be extremely severe, it is the shelter provided by tall Scots pines and oaks on the steep sides of a natural dell that has enabled Lady Anne to make a garden containing a number of tender varieties. When Lady Anne bought Broadleas in 1946 the old gardens around the house had fallen into decay and the dell was more rough woodland than part of the garden. In her replanting of the areas around the house Lady Anne has certainly enhanced their original pre-war appearance, but it has been in the creation of her woodland garden in the dell—which drops away from the far side of the large lawn beyond the south-facing front of the house—that she has been most successful.

As well as the protective canopy of the mature trees and its naturally sheltering shape the dell slopes away to one end, thereby minimizing the danger of becoming a frost pocket. Another important factor is the greensand soil ideally suited to the trees and shrubs Lady Anne is most interested in. Among the more tender plants which benefit from the shelter are a collection of unusual rhododendrons, eucryphias and *Crinodendron hookeranum*, which has brilliant red flowers like hanging lanterns. Throughout the dell are numerous ornamental trees: stewartia, davidia, cercidiphyllum, styrax and nissa, of which the best group are the magnolias. Near the top of the dell towards the lawn and house beyond *Magnolia sargentiana*, *M. sargentiana* 'Robusta', *M.*

Maenan. Looking across the dell with rhododendrons and other plants growing informally below the sheltering mature trees.

cylindrica and *M. sprengeri* 'Diva' make an impressive greeting too.

Besides the many interesting and unusual individuals in the dell Lady Anne has given it a broader woodland character with quantities of spring bulbs: daffodils, anemones and primroses, and more rarified erythroniums, and spreading herbaceous groundcover plants. If the appearance is at times exotic—especially in spring and early summer—the style is quite natural as emphasized by the manner in which the lie of the land continues unbroken from the dell into the meadows beyond.

Following the death in 1953 of the 2nd Lord Aberconway his widow moved from Bodnant to the family's nearby house of Maenan. There she—and subsequently her son Christopher McLaren who now lives there—have created a garden largely inspired by the family masterpiece nearby. As at Bodnant the garden has an outstanding setting, and at the far end from the house is the dell, where a woodland garden has been made beneath the protective canopy of oak, ash and sycamore. The dell's sloping sides provide a dramatic background for the new planting, in particular the bank of camellias beneath a steep cliff and the quantity of deciduous azaleas planted in a natural bowl on another side. Since 1980 the dell has been extended across the drive leading to the house into a glade planted with a collection of rhododendrons and various ornamental trees.

Since the Second World War the woodland garden has unquestionably proved the most successful and widely popular medium in which to apply the natural style that has become one of the main threads of British gardening. This style provides the ideal surroundings for many of the ornamental trees and shrubs that have now become widely available, as opposed to being the prized possessions of a limited number of gardens as they were in the past. A woodland garden, as well as offering enormous possibilities to an aspiring plantsman, can be developed at whatever pace is wished and, once properly established, can be largely self-maintaining.

8
PLANTSMAN'S PARADISE

Sylvia Crowe maintains that throughout history the role of plants in a garden has been thought of in one of two ways: either the purpose of a garden is to grow plants, or plants are one of a number of materials to be used in making a garden.[1] Encouraged by the greatly increased availability of all types of plant and by more widespread knowledge of them, the majority of British gardeners since the war held to the first approach. There has, however, been a tendency also for the two threads to become joined, so that it is plants alone which provide both the detail of a garden and the overall picture of it. At times this has led to confusion, with plants being used in such a frenetic manner that any harmony in the garden's structure is obscured, a situation which Russell Page compares to imagining the Parthenon with each of its columns made from a different kind of marble.[2]

On the other hand, this ascendant position enjoyed by plants of one kind or another has produced a number of gardens of absorbing interest: in some cases where it is one type or even one genus that is the particular speciality; in others the use of a wide variety succeeds in balancing the individual qualities of the plants with successful grouping and a satisfying overall structure. This in turn has also influenced the development of more general tendencies: the use of striking ornamental trees and shrubs as focal points or the central feature of a design, instead of architectural features or statuary such as pavilions, statues or urns; and, in recent years, a growing interest in some species of little known native British plants and their more widespread use in gardens. Since 1978 this has been encouraged by the National Council for the Preservation of Plants and Gardens, which has, at the same time, underlined the rarity and threatened status of many of these plants.

Plantsmanship has become an admired and sought-after talent. For many gardeners, the raising and tending of difficult or unusual plants, or the building up of a 'collection'—be it of trees with striking autumn foliage, shrub roses or alpines—are their primary source of enjoyment. Greenhouses and small electric propagators have introduced people to horticultural secrets and delights that, in the past, were the jealously guarded domain of head gardeners and nurserymen.

Perhaps most important, the pursuit of horticultural excellence is ideally suited to the reduced scale on which most people are gardening nowadays. Where there is neither the space for grand design nor the labour for intensive maintenance the use of plants is of paramount importance and, where it is successful, can give a relatively small garden concentrated interest in inverse proportion to its overall size. Certainly Miles Hadfield was accurate when he concluded, at the end of the revised edition of *A History of British Gardening* (1979), that 'The rapid increase in the number of small houses has brought into being a large new class of often highly intelligent and enthusiastic plantsmen. The future of gardening in Britain is largely in their hands.'[3]

The small scale of the garden of the Dower House, Boughton in Northamptonshire, for example, is accentuated by the grandiose setting of parkland that surrounds Boughton House, a seat of the Duke of Buccleuch and of which the Dower House forms the east wing. The garden has been made since the Second World War in two stages, from 1948 to 1965 by Sir David Scott, a cousin of the Duke's, and his first wife (who died in 1965), and subsequently by Sir David and his second wife, Valerie Finnis, whom he married in 1970. He himself died in 1986, aged ninety-nine. One description of the Dower House garden as developed by Sir David and Valerie Finnis is as complimentary an acknowledgment as any plantsman's garden could hope for: 'This is a garden of especial interest to the horticulturally well-informed, for the care that has been taken to include only the best plants is matched by the skill exercised in finding them the most congenial locations from a cultural point of view. This is, therefore, a garden in which to observe and learn as well as to enjoy its purely visual attractions.'[4]

The clear division of the garden into three areas allowed Sir David and the second Lady Scott to indulge independently their own preferences, his for trees and shrubs and hers for alpines and other small plants of which she had previously built up a notable collection at the Waterperry School of Horticulture, near Oxford. Much of this collection went with her to Boughton in 1970 and has since been greatly expanded.

The garden that Sir David and his first wife had inherited from his parents, and began work on after his retirement from the Foreign Office in 1947, initially covered only two of the three areas: the small enclosed courtyard immediately below the elegant south front of the house, and a smaller rectangular vegetable garden on a higher level across a wide entrance yard. Sir David's wish to grow trees and shrubs led him to take in also a piece of ground beyond the vegetable garden. This was on the edge of the Boughton park and had been kept in trim by deer until shortly after the turn of the century when they were fenced out and the site became a wilderness. Once all the brambles and other undergrowth had been cleared the new area gave the garden a total of two acres.

The keynote throughout is the quantity of rare and unusual plants. Some one would not expect to see outside far milder parts of the country, others are little

The Dower House, Boughton. Grass paths wind among the richly planted beds in the part of the garden that was always Sir David Scott's domain.

known or 'difficult' members of well-established families. The individual needs, characteristics and qualities of each plant are of primary importance and yet through sensitive grouping and association it is always a garden and not just a collection; or, as the Scotts themselves have described it, 'a home for plants'.[5]

The warm, south-facing front of the house supports a mixture of climbers and wall-plants—roses and clematis joining with choice plants originating from overseas. In front of the house, in beds filled to overflowing and divided by paved paths, tender shrubs mix with hardy perennials, all thickly underplanted with foliage specialities. Further interest in this smallest area of the garden is given by stone sinks and troughs, filled with the small plants which are Lady Scott's especial delight and giving a notion of what lies ahead in the old vegetable garden. Here, while fruit and vegetables have been retained in much of the central area, the boundaries of the walled-in rectangle have been made into raised beds against the walls, constructed with railway sleepers and totalling over two hundred yards in length around the four sides. A distinction has been made between the long south-facing and north-facing beds, the former being for alpines which thrive in warmth and full sun, the latter filled with imported peat and acid-based soil to accommodate, among other things, small shade-loving plants, otherwise found in a woodland setting, such as trilliums, erythroniums and hellebores. The raised beds have now annexed part of the central area from the vegetables and at one end is the production area of greenhouses and frames whence originate the large majority of the inhabitants of the raised beds.

The largest area is that taken in from the park by Sir David and was his domain—principally of trees and shrubs planted in a series of informally arranged island beds divided by wandering grass paths. Each bed has a name and a particular theme and there are now between eighty and one hundred of them. Some of the trees and shrubs planted in the early days are now approaching—or have grown to—maturity, and additional interest is provided by spring bulbs and summer herbaceous plants beneath. Sir David freely admitted that this part of the garden was made without an overall plan, rather it expanded in a fairly random fashion as the undergrowth was tamed. In addition to the clearing that needed to be done the site had the limitations of a north-facing aspect and an alkaline soil over heavy clay. As a result lime-loving plants—such as prunus, viburnums, daphnes and smaller dianthus—are especially evident along with, for instance, extensive collections of acers and willows—many of the latter pollarded for their red and orange shoots in the winter—while there are none of the rhododendrons so often found in such an informal semi-woodland setting.

The best and simplest way to summarize the quality of the Dower House garden is by quoting the Scotts' description of their garden, written some time before Sir David's death:

> The main feature of the garden, which is looked after by us with occasional outside help (we have no regular gardener), is the wide variety of shrubs and plants and bulbs which it contains. It was not laid out on a plan and any apparent design is purely accidental. The well-being of the plants has always been the primary consideration and we regard it as a home for plants rather than a garden. It has, however, the merit of being full of surprises and its general appearance is greatly improved by the slight

undulations in the ground. Except for the lack of ericaceous shrubs it has, we think, something to interest a keen plantsman at any time of the year.[6]

This description could almost be applied to the Garden House, Buckland Monochorum, in Devon, where Lionel Fortescue began making the garden in 1945, after spending many years as a schoolmaster at Eton. Right up to his death in 1981 he was a ruthless perfectionist about what he allowed to grow in his garden and, to his gardening friends, notoriously acquisitive of plants which he coveted. One of his tricks was to return to a garden he was visiting after being shown round, on the pretence of collecting a dropped handkerchief, only surreptitiously to pocket a small cutting of some speciality he liked. In his own garden weaklings were not tolerated and as a result the quantities of plants there displayed unusual vigour and good health throughout the year. After his death the Fortescue Garden Trust was set up to safeguard the garden's survival into the future and Fortescue's own high standard is maintained by Keith Wiley, the head gardener for many years while he was alive.

The house is well named as the garden surrounds it on all sides and extends in one direction where the sloping ground has been made into a series of descending terraces. The terraces probably date from when the abbot of

The Dower House, Boughton. The south-facing raised bed filled with sun-loving alpines and other small plants.

Buckland Abbey moved to the then vicarage on the site, after the Dissolution of the Monasteries. Other than this basic structure everything in the garden dates from after the Second World War. Initially the most important necessity was to give some protection, for the main slope is exposed and faces the south-west side of Dartmoor. In addition to the old walls which enclose some of one side and most of the lower area, hedges of Leyland cypress were added, in particular one stretching down the slope on one side of the garden. Other hedges—of cotoneaster, thuja and pittosporum—give further protection by dividing the areas of the terraces. The lowest area had obviously been a kitchen garden and the acid soil to be found in the rest of the garden had been modified there by generations of vegetables so that lime-tolerant plants could be grown.

The changing terrain of the garden and its divisions formed by the terraces and hedges provide the ideal setting for the great variety of plants which give interest through most of the year. The lowest walled area, which contains an old barn and the remains of a small tower, is given over mainly to herbaceous plants. Above are the terraces where more herbaceous plants are mixed with predominant shrubs and many outstanding ornamental or flowering trees. On one narrow terrace is *Eucryphia milliganii* and above, in borders around the lawn on the largest terrace, *Eucryphia glutinosa* and *Hoheria glabrata*, the latter from New Zealand and testifying to the degree of shelter achieved in the garden. On one of the upper terraces is the best of the garden's magnolias, *Magnolia salicifolia* and, close by, a spectacular bank of massed *Camellia japonicas*. Camellias are certainly a feature of the garden, and a similarly bold planting of 'Donation' greets visitors near the entrance.

With camellias, the other outstanding group of shrubs in the garden is rhododendrons. One large mixed group fills a triangular space made by two of the cypress hedges; to one side of the terraces and above the house a bank is closely planted with mixed azaleas and rhododendrons. Perhaps the most interesting of the rhododendrons are two hybrids raised by Lionel Fortescue himself at the Garden House, one named 'Katherine Fortescue' after his wife, which was given an Award of Merit by the Royal Horticultural Society in 1981, the other named 'Lionel Fortescue'. Both have brilliant yellow flowers. It is characteristic of Lionel Fortescue's approach that his garden is particularly strong in yellow rhododendrons, their most elusive pure colour.

In most places the trees and shrubs are underplanted with a correspondingly varied array of smaller plants, such as the pink erythroniums and fritillaries above the house. There are constant reminders of the degree of shelter which has been achieved, not least the white-flowered *Clematis indivisa* on one wall of the house, a very tender climber hailing also from the far milder climate of New Zealand and rarely seen in England outside a greenhouse or conservatory. Covering the wall next to the clematis is a harmoniously white wisteria. Associations such as this, as well as the bold grouping, particularly of

Marwood Hill. Both sides of the stream are densely planted with iris, primulas, lysichitums and other aquatic plants.

rhododendrons and camellias, are additional features of a garden where, as at the Dower House, the major consideration is the quality of individual plants. In recent years this has been extended to an excellent nursery that offers many of the rarer varieties to be found thriving in the garden.

On the other side of Devon, close to Barnstaple and within a few miles of the county's north-west coast, is the garden of Marwood Hill, begun by its owner, Dr James Smart, in 1960. The garden has expanded ever since. It now extends to twelve acres and, Dr Smart estimates, contains over three thousand different varieties of plants. He originally lived in the fine Georgian house across the lane and it is a measure of his gardening commitment that he did not site and build his new house until much of his garden had been planned and planted, thereby ensuring the ideal vantage point. The site of the garden is a long valley with a stream flowing along the bottom which, in 1969, was dammed in different places to form three lakes. The house is positioned at the top of the slope on one side, its windows giving views over virtually the whole of the garden as it extends away down the valley.

126

The general style is open and informal, with larger trees and shrubs planted in open grass with mown paths leading amongst them, and smaller ones in different beds mulched with crushed bark. Two important priorities for Dr Smart have always been that the garden should merge easily into the surrounding landscape of sheep meadows on the far side of the valley from the house and woodland at the bottom end of the stream, and that the trees and shrubs which predominate should be arranged not only for their individual advantage, but also to allow the views and vistas which the sloping terrain provides. Many of the plants are treasures collected by Dr Smart on trips abroad, especially from Australia, New Zealand and Tasmania. On the level ground of the old walled garden, which originally belonged to Dr Smart's old house, he has built a large glasshouse filled with tender plants from this part of the world which he calls the Australia House. On the far side of the valley a collection of eucalyptus have been planted with birches to show how easily they integrate with many native trees.

Along the outside of the high lower wall of the walled garden, whose regular buttresses are ideal for the training of climbers, and which faces south across the valley, Dr Smart has planted a selection of tender plants as well as many small-flowered clematis. There are acacias from Australia, and a number of ceanothus, with roses mixing freely with the more tender visitors. Below the terrace walk along the wall there is a newly made raised scree bed for alpines, which originally grew in an old quarry at one end of the garden.

Beyond the walled garden is a large area, the most recently planted, which is essentially an ornamental woodland. Trees and shrubs, notable for either their flowers or their foliage, are planted individually between bold grass rides which cut vistas up and down the slope, many of them focusing from the bottom on the tall church tower which stands sentinel on top of the rise, across the road from the walled garden. The entrances to the rides are marked by fastigiate trees and it is particularly interesting to see such an extensively planted area at a young age, and imagine how it will look once the trees and shrubs have grown to maturity leaving the rides cutting vistas between them.

The edges of the lakes are closely planted with iris, arum lilies, lysichitums and other aquatic varieties and, at regular intervals, there are a number of trees judiciously positioned to catch the eye: *Picea brewerana*, the slow-growing 'Brewer's Weeping Spruce', *Prunus Shirotae* 'Mount Fuji' and *Cercidiphyllum japonicum* with outstanding autumn colour. The smaller plants continue along the edges of the stream leading out of the lowest lake, planted in places with quantities of candelabra primulas. At the far end of the stream, where it flows out of the garden into the neighbouring wood, Dr Smart's enjoyment of landscape in the grand manner has produced the newly-built architectural trio of a hump-backed bridge over the stream, with, nearby, a seat beneath a metal arbour covered with scented climbers and, on the edge of the garden, a circular folly of eight pillars enclosing an eighteenth-century lead cherub.

Across the main lake from the house, the far slope offers perhaps the most striking mixture of planting in the garden. Collections of magnolias and rhododendrons are planted together, including unusual varieties of both: *Magnolia dawsoniana* and *Rhododendron macabeanum*, as well as camellias, which are among Dr Smart's favourites, embothriums and eucryphias. To one side a group of firs leads up the slope to *Abies spectabilis* whose seed Dr Smart collected in Nepal. Close to the lake a small but effective group is made by Acer 'Senkaki' and a silver weeping pear with two clematis trained into its branches.

Although, for the time being, the garden at Marwood Hill appears to have stopped expanding in size, new additions and changes are constantly being made, such as two small coppices planted in the field opposite the house outside the garden's boundaries. If the garden is characteristically modern in its flowing informality and extensive use of ornamental trees and shrubs, these are features that are not only well suited to the site but have also enabled Dr Smart to maintain the garden with only limited help.

Dr Smart's closest gardening neighbour is Lady Anne Palmer. Her garden at Rosemoor, near Torrington, is roughly the same age and certainly of a similar calibre to Marwood Hill. Although Lady Anne and her late husband had lived in the white Georgian house since just after the war, it was not until the late 1950s that she embarked upon creating the present garden. Her enthusiasm was partly fired by meeting Captain Collingwood 'Cherry' Ingram, then aged eighty. Captain Ingram, the maestro of the Japanese cherry, who died in 1980 aged a hundred, gave Lady Anne an initial interest in gardening and plant-collecting which she has retained ever since.

The garden at Rosemoor has steadily extended away from the south-facing front of the house, along a valley protected by wooded hills above the garden to the north and east. It is as much a collector's garden as a plantsman's—or rather, plantswoman's—and many of the unusual trees and shrubs with which it abounds have been grown from seed collected in the wild by Lady Anne. This is especially true of the large arboretum, at the south end of the garden, where planting began in 1975. The garden contains a number of specialities: hollies, of which Lady Anne now has over one hundred different plants; cherries, of course, through Captain Ingram's influence, and the National Collection of cornus; but these are mixed with a now considerable array of different plants. Many of the larger trees and shrubs grow free-standing on the lawns around the house or in longer mown grass, while others have been effectively positioned to give height to the series of large, informally shaped island beds to one side of the drive which sweeps away from the house and divides the garden. These beds lead to a large pond and on the other side of the drive, a long bed is devoted mainly to rhododendrons. Rare plants and peculiarities are everywhere—in one place a fastigiate copper beech. This was originally a

Broadleas. The dell in spring.

The Dower House, Boughton. Abundant planting in the garden
immediately in front of the house.

The Garden House, Buckland Monochorum. Delicate pink *Erythronium revolutum*.

Marwood Hill. The view from the house across the main lake to
informal planting of trees and shrubs on the far side.

The Garden House, Buckland Monochorum. Looking through one of the hedges in the lowest part of the garden.

seedling from a Dawyck beech at the famous Trompenberg Arboretum near Rotterdam, whence a number of other trees in the garden have originated. As well as the individual qualities of each specimen, grouping is carefully arranged, as in one of the beds where mixed herbaceous plants surround *Rhododendron* 'Crest', probably the best yellow-flowered rhododendron hybrid and raised at Exbury by Lionel de Rothschild.

Elsewhere in the garden a hard tennis court has been ingeniously replaced by a gravel garden, with beds of earth laid on the court surface and filled with a collection of dwarf conifers. In 1973 the old kitchen garden was replanned with the help of John Codrington. As well as many shrub roses it now contains two raised beds—one with acid soil, the other with alkaline, as at the Dower House—filled with alpines. Where the garden merges into the wooded hillside above, some trees have been cleared and replaced with rhododendrons and other plants suited to a woodland habitat. Rosemoor is in the tradition of collectors' gardens and its interest is especially botanical and horticultural, each plant being meticulously labelled and its details recorded. At the same time its whole style is geared towards low maintenance—an important consideration in a garden which contains such a large number of plants and now extends to

Rosemoor. The gravel garden with its varied conifers which has replaced the tennis court.

nearly eleven acres. In 1987 it was announced that Lady Anne had donated the garden to the Royal Horticultural Society.

At the Priory, Kemerton in Worcestershire, trees and shrubs play only a very minor role in a garden the inspiration for which derived from William Robinson's *The English Flower Garden*. This was the only book Peter Healing possessed while he was in Germany at the end of the war. It was then that he sketched out the plans for his garden of which the major features were to be a series of herbaceous borders planted principally with an eye to carefully blended colour sequences. While the lay-out of the four-acre garden has changed little from Peter Healing's original draft, the borders which he has made have been progressively and discerningly filled with both traditional and unusual herbaceous and other perennial plants. As much as any other garden the Priory maintains the tradition of border plantsmanship established by Robinson and Jekyll, at the same time as containing many plants from abroad which they are unlikely to have known.

The main area of planting lies to one side of the attractive, eighteenth-century stone house. Three rectangular herbaceous borders have been made. One stretches away from the house with a picturesque sixteenth-century ruin and a huge, ancient yew tree behind, the other two are at right angles to this and divided by mown lawn. Each border has its own distinct appearance and character, while in all of them the overriding factor has been colour combination. The most striking border is the one that leads away from the house which is planted exclusively with shades of red extending into oranges and purples. Behind the herbaceous plants are bushes of purple berberis and cotinus and, mixing with flowering plants, are many with striking foliage, such as ornamental beetroot.

The Priory, Kemerton. Looking across the lawns and borders.

At right angles, and facing the house, is the smaller of the two mixed borders, free-standing, so to speak, with lawn on all sides, and filled with plants of pastel shades—white, pink, mauve and soft blue. Mixing with the predominant herbaceous plants are annuals and white shrub roses and, as in the other borders, there are a number of rarely seen members of well-known families. From the house, the main border lies behind this one, separated by lawn, and is of impressive proportions—over fifty yards long and eighteen feet deep. Here the colours of the plants are seen against the dark green tones of a yew hedge. It is in this main border that Peter Healing's progression of colour is most successfully displayed. From one end of the border groups of white and silver plants blend into pale pink and then pale yellow, whence the shades of the dominant groups become progressively brighter and 'hotter', through stronger yellow to bronze and orange to red in the centre, and then fade away again to the border's far end. The effect is achieved not only by the careful arrangement of colour, but by using large enough groups of plants to ensure that each dominant colour is a bold statement. Behind roses and other shrubs, clematis trained over wooden supports and giant silver thistles give the necessary sense of height.

From one end of the border a long wooden pergola draped with roses and vines—of which Gertrude Jekyll would certainly have approved—leads away from the house. Along here is the surprise discovery of a secluded garden, enclosed on two sides by the yew hedge, which backs the main border and continues along the far side from the pergola, and on the other sides by tall trees and shrubs. This garden, not thought of until later than the main borders, was conceived by Peter Healing to 'fill the gap between spring bulbs and blossom and the high summer display of the herbaceous borders.'[7] Wide double borders are divided only by a narrow line of round flagstones and filled with plants of pastel shades of flower and leaf—silver, white, pink and mauve. When they are in full flower the borders almost engulf the flags which lead to a stone vase mounted on a low pedestal. The satisfaction provided by the overall picture of this small area, and the mixture of plants and of their colour and habit would have been appreciated by Peter Healing's mentor and, possibly more than the main borders and the other areas of the garden, show a balance between artistry and plantsmanship.

Peter Wake is descended from the Holford family who planted the arboretum at Westonbirt. If he continues the horticultural enthusiasm of his forebears, his garden of four acres on chalky Hampshire soil at Fairfield House, Hambledon, is very different in both scale and content. The garden was not begun until 1970 and an important consideration was always that it should be maintainable by Peter Wake and his wife. The garden is mainly given over to a collection of old-fashioned and specie shrub roses and climbers. In front of the white Regency house and to one side large cedars of Lebanon, limes and beech (both copper

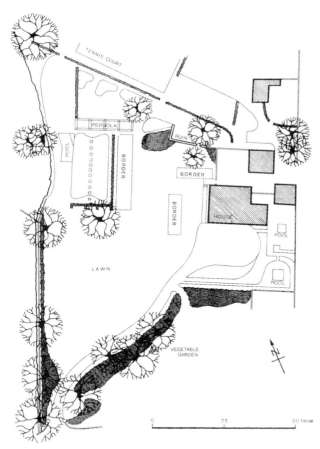

The Priory, Kemerton. A plan of the garden designed and planted by Peter Healing.

Fairfield House. A quiet bench overhung with climbing roses.

and green) were planted shortly after it was built, and spread their canopies over open lawn. While the walls of the house and the slender pillars of the veranda on these two sides support climbing roses, the main areas of development have been in the old two-acre walled kitchen garden to the north of the house and in a smaller walled enclosure on the east side.

Once the walled garden had been cleared, the main area was grassed and planted with ornamental—mainly flowering—trees, in an orchard style; malus, prunus, crataegus and sorbus as well as a metasequoia and a Dawyck beech. Mown grass paths wind between areas of longer grass while mixing with the trees is a carefully chosen selection of shrub roses, planted individually and trained over wooden supports to display their habit and flowers to the best advantage. Among the most striking are *californica* 'Plena', 'Complicata' and 'Margaret Hilling', all with pink flowers, the Gallicas 'Belle de Crécy' and 'Tuscany Superb' and the white-flowered 'Maxima', 'Céleste' and 'Mme Plantier'. More shrubs are closely and contrastingly planted along one side, beneath the brick wall swathed in climbing and rambling varieties.

More roses have helped to incorporate an oval swimming pool and tennis court into the walled garden. At one end of the pool a brick pergola and the walls on either side of a small pavilion support the climbers 'François Juranville', 'The Garland', 'Mme Grégoire Strachelin', 'Rambling Rector' and 'Albertine', while 'Félicité et Perpétue' is trained into the wires around the court. In the smaller walled area to the east of the house roses are again in the majority, but here they are mixed with other shrubs and spreading santolinas and helichrysums below. The meticulous attention that the roses receive throughout the year, ensuring that their summer flowering period is a spectacular sight, has given the garden a feeling of maturity which its age would not suggest.

With roses, perhaps camellias and rhododendrons have absorbed more gardeners than any other species—especially those in the south-west of England. Major-General Eric Harrison's garden at Tremeer near the north coast of Cornwall was begun in 1947 and now contains outstanding collections of both plants, even by the standards of some of its illustrious older neighbours. In fact it was the closest of these established gardens, Lamellen, which was partly responsible for giving General Harrison his initial gardening enthusiasm. When he bought Tremeer in 1939 he was more interested in the hunting but within a few months the outbreak of war had put an end to any such plans. It was only after his return at the end of the war that he was able to turn his attention to gardening. The hostilities provided him with a useful short-term labour force in the shape of German prisoners of war whom he called in to help replace the fir trees along the drive with the present flowering cherries.

General Harrison determined from an early stage both to grow camellias and rhododendrons in his own garden, and to breed new hybrids. At Tremeer the existing garden site consisted of a terrace along the south front of the house, lawn covered in undergrowth, a decaying orchard and wood beyond. He decided to retain the basic structure, leaving the terrace descending to lawn with the main areas of planting beyond. The garden was fairly well sheltered by trees around the boundaries and in front of the house. One important improvement was to clear and extend the pond in one corner of the woodland into a small lake out of which the water flows into a stream that winds along the garden's bottom edge.

In 1961 General Harrison married Roza Stevenson who, with her first husband, had built up a famous collection of rhododendrons at their home, Tower Court, near Ascot. After her husband's death the majority of the collection was transferred to the Savill Gardens in Windsor Great Park. However, she brought a number of outstanding plants to Tremeer where they were replanted, most notably the collection of original Kurume evergreen azaleas from Japan. These were placed in two large new beds made on either side of the central steps leading from the terrace at Tremeer to the lawn. The original plant of the striking yellow rhododendron 'Damaris Logan' from Tower Court survives at Tremeer, close to another with yellow flowers named 'Roza Stevenson' after her, which was awarded a First Class Certificate by the Royal Horticultural Society in 1968.

Evidence of General Harrison's successful raising of hybrids can be seen throughout the garden. The main lawn leads to banks of blue and mauve rhododendrons which mark the edge of the woodland garden and include two of his best 'Breward' and 'St Tudy', the latter named after the tiny village close to Tremeer. Shaded by trees to one side of the lake is a plant of the most delicate rhododendron he raised, 'Belle of Tremeer', with silvery-blue flowers standing close to the equally refined *Rh. schlippenbachii*.

Across the lake a plant of Camellia 'Donation' has been positioned as an eye-catcher beneath the taller trees and both here and elsewhere it is one of the most rewarding camellias among the two-hundred-plus different plants in the garden. Beyond one corner of the main lawn a number of plants has been grouped close together to form a great bank and a wide selection of different varieties has been planted on the raised bank behind the house.

As well as its two mainstays Tremeer has also been given a more varied character by a mixture of trees and shrubs that blend in successfully with the rhododendrons and camellias. Some, such as the acers 'Atropurpureum' 'Osakazuki' and 'Griseum', and *Magnolia veitchii*, are strategically positioned among the paths which wander through the woodland areas. Along the stream are quantities of candelabra primulas.

For General Harrison gardening was many-faceted. Not only did he make the garden at Tremeer, but he also bred plants and exhibited at competitions.

This was perhaps why, in 1978, he decided to leave Tremeer, since when it has been owned by Dr Haslam and Mrs Hopwood. General Harrison was certainly someone who believed that a garden was for growing plants and yet, like many of the best plantsmen, he succeeded in making a garden of both specialist interest and visual beauty. While such gardens are sometimes threatened by the loss of their creators, they will assuredly continue to appear and to reflect the strong trend towards the achievement of horticultural excellence in gardens created since the Second World War.

9
RE-CREATING THE PAST

It is often difficult to make the distinction between what is a new garden and one that is essentially a reconstruction. Many gardens created since the war have been made on the sites of old ones, some features of which—trees, walls or even a basic lay-out—often survive. There are, however, a number of gardens that are either ambitious and important restorations of historical gardens—which had suffered extensive decay and been threatened with extinction—or that are faithful re-creations in the style of a past period. Conservation and preservation have become especially powerful words in the gardening context in recent decades and the interest, both nostalgic and practical, that the riches of Britain's gardening past evoke is greater and more influential than ever before.

More than any other, it is the gardens of the seventeenth century and earlier which arouse the most sympathetic response today, because of their rarity as a result of the destruction they suffered at the hands of the eighteenth-century landscape movement. And while the qualities of those landscapes are now undisputed, few people today would look upon their own gardens in such an expansive manner. Far more appealing is the intimacy, the smaller scale, the intricate design and use of traditional plants that is associated with the Tudors and Stuarts. The ornamental herb and knot gardens which are now so popular draw their inspiration from this period and many of them take their plans and planting straight from gardening or botanical books of that time.

Fittingly, one of the grandest Jacobean houses in the country, Hatfield House, has in recent years acquired gardens ambitiously re-created to evoke the character and reveal the style of their original period. The re-creation is the work of the present Marchioness of Salisbury who, working within the basic structure of the gardens which have evolved steadily since the house was built by Robert Cecil, first Earl of Salisbury, between 1607 and 1611, has given them a character and appearance that combines a flavour of the Italian Renaissance, which had begun to affect English gardens by the beginning of the seventeenth century, with that of older Tudor gardens. The success of Lady Salisbury's work has been made possible partly by her knowledge of gardening during the sixteenth and seventeenth centuries, and in particular of the plants collected and used by John Tradescant the Elder, for many years Robert Cecil's gardener.

The Tudor influence is most deliberately shown in the sunken area of garden

Hatfield House. The new maze and knot garden in front of the remaining wing of the Tudor palace of Hatfield.

in front of the remaining wing of the old Palace of Hatfield, which once formed a quadrangle around this area and was where the young Princess Elizabeth, after many years of semi-imprisonment, first heard that she was queen. A Victorian rose garden has been taken out and in its place Lady Salisbury has laid out a maze of clipped box hedges and gravel and a larger knot garden, divided into sections by brick cross-paths leading to a central fountain. In addition to the box hedges that enclose the beds of the knot garden, spirals of holly on the corners add to the period formality. Most important, only plants known to have been used in the fifteenth, sixteenth and seventeenth centuries have been planted in the knot garden, where, among the random mixture, there are extensive collections of old tulips, dianthus, violas and narcissus.

To one side of the knot garden, below the west front of the house, a parterre garden has been made on the site of what was, centuries ago, a Tudor privy garden. Yew hedges enclose a square where the pattern of beds has been taken from a plan dated 1497 relating to gardens around the old palace. Outside the yew hedges are pleached lime walks on all sides. While the planting is as historically selective as in the knot garden the mixture of roses, other shrubs and flowering and foliage herbaceous plants achieves a similarly effusive effect.

An opening through the pleached limes on the far side from the house leads to the scented garden where different plants give a progression of fragrance through the year: chimonanthus in winter, daphnes and philadelphus in spring and early summer and, later, old-fashioned roses, honeysuckle and tobacco plants. Within the scented garden is a herb garden, its patterned beds of herbs divided by paved paths in which camomile and thyme have been deliberately planted so as to produce their scent when trodden on, recalling the words of the Elizabethan philosopher, essayist and gardener, Francis Bacon: 'But those which perfume the air most delightfully, not passed by as the rest, but being trodden upon and crushed are three: that is burnet, wild thyme, and water-mints. Therefore you are to set whole alleys of them, to have the pleasure when you walk or tread.'[1]

It is to the east of the house that the influence of the Renaissance is most evident. The grand terrace along the front of the house, whose stone balustrading supports seventeenth-century Italian statues, looks down on to a series of large, square, box-edged beds set into lawn. The main sweep of grass across the centre of the garden stretches between more statues. The planting in the beds is mainly old-fashioned roses, but with a characteristic mixture of other plants as well. On either side the garden is enclosed by gravel paths flanked by rows of standard ilex trees, their slender trunks supporting neatly clipped domes. Beyond this garden, on lower terraces, are older established features such as the nineteenth-century maze.

Further additions to the gardens at Hatfield will be a kitchen garden along seventeenth-century lines and a grassed 'broad walk' between holly hedges. Already, Lady Salisbury has skilfully achieved her ambition to, 'make the garden more closely connected to and harmonious with the house, as it would have been when the house was originally built and the garden made in the early seventeenth century'.[2]

Like Hatfield, Helmingham Hall in Suffolk is the home of a family with famous Tudor and Stuart ancestors—the Tollemaches. The house is older, dating from 1510, and one of the most evocative in England, built around a courtyard and protected on all sides by a broad moat. There have been gardens to the south of the house ever since it was built and in the large walled garden, enclosed during the 1740s, squares of fruit and vegetables are divided by impressive double herbaceous borders flanking long grass paths between wrought-iron gateways. Here, and in the parterre garden, surrounded by borders of shrub roses, which lies between the walled garden and the house, the present Lord and Lady Tollemache have only made alterations to the planting.

Beyond the far, north, side of the house it is a very different story. Since 1982 a sunken area of two acres has been transformed from grass that merged uninterestingly into the surrounding parkland into a pattern of formally laid out herb and knot gardens, and an Elizabethan rose garden, triumphantly in keeping with the architectural period of the house. To some extent the inspiration for the new garden came from Lord and Lady Tollemache's ambition to create out of a 'dead' area something which lived up to the old 'Elizabethan' gardens on the other side of the house. These had recently

Helmingham Hall. Looking down on to the new garden from the house.

become one of only two gardens in Suffolk to be accorded Grade I status by English Heritage, in their *Register of Parks and Gardens of special historic interest in England*. In planning the garden they were helped by Lady Salisbury, whose work at Hatfield—and indeed, also at Cranborne in Dorset, the family's second home—has given her a considerable and deserved reputation.

The lay-out of the new garden is ideally simple. The rectangular area is enclosed on three sides by yew hedges. From the house the grass terrace along the moat is broken in the centre by a flight of brick steps which leads down to a wide grass path stretching right through the centre of the garden. Immediately below the terrace are the knot and herb gardens, on either side of the central path, each containing four symmetrically arranged square beds. Beyond here rectangular beds on either side, filled with hedges of the striped pink *Rosa* 'mundii' underplanted with banks of catmint, mark the division with the rose garden beyond. Here the beds form a large square with the four main outside beds cut away in the middle by a circular grass path surrounding smaller curving beds and a central classical statue from Lady Salisbury's garden centre at Cranborne. In line with the statue, paths lead out of the garden at right angles to the main one—in one direction to wrought-iron gates and the swimming pool hidden away beyond, and in the other to the fine Georgian coach house which faces the garden.

Ham House. The parterre of box-edged beds of cotton lavender, restored by the National Trust.

Much of the success of such an ambitious project has derived from Lord and Lady Tollemache's enthusiasm and enterprise. All of the old bricks, which neatly enclose the various beds and form also the steps up to the terrace and the path to the coach house come from the Helmingham estate itself. Similarly the yards of box hedging used in the knot and herb gardens are all plants grown from cuttings made in the garden. Already, after only a few years, the garden's considerable charm is immediately evident. In the knot garden the initials 'T' and 'A' (for Lord and Lady Tollemache's christian names, Timothy and Alexandra) join with the Tollemache fret—the family crest—to form the knots within which are a host of small traditional flowers. Opposite, in the herb garden, the herbs are similarly arranged in patterns.

The beds of the rose garden are edged with 'Hidcote' lavender and in each of the four main ones old-fashioned shrub roses are arranged by family: Specie and Albas in one, Centifolia and Moss in another, Gallicas, Damasks and Bourbons in the third and, in the fourth, Rugosas, Chinas and Hybrid Perpetuals. The conditions are obviously most suitable as the shrubs have attained healthy size and are mixed with foxgloves, penstemons and other old-fashioned herbaceous plants.

140

For many centuries the Tollemaches had another family seat at Ham House, Richmond. Since 1948 Ham has been a property of the National Trust which, in recent years, has completed an exciting reconstruction of the gardens which had entirely disappeared. They had been described admiringly, however, by John Evelyn three hundred years earlier: 'The Parterres, Flower Gardens, Orangeries, Groves, Avenues, Courts, Statues, Perspectives, Fountains, Aviaries, and all this on the banks of the Sweetest River in the World must needs be surprising.'[3]

Now many of the features so admired by Evelyn have returned to Ham House. Beyond the garden front of the house what was a vast unkempt lawn has been divided again into a pattern of square 'plats' and is enclosed by lime avenues on either side. Below the terrace in front of the house is a long border devoted only to rosemary and different coloured sages. Beyond the plats of lawn what was a patch of overgrown woodland has been restored to a wilderness, as it would originally have been, with serpentine paths winding among the trees. Most striking of all is the reconstructed knot garden to one side of the house. A box-edged parterre of diagonal beds covers an area of 1,800 square yards, the beds divided by gravel paths. All of the beds are filled with massed domes of silvery-grey cotton lavender. The diagonal lines of the pattern are accentuated by pyramids of clipped box at intervals along the low hedges.

Since acquiring Hidcote in 1948 the National Trust has become the curator and guardian of well over one hundred gardens. In this capacity, and given its enormous resources compared to most private owners of gardens, it is in a unique position to restore gardens such as the one at Ham House and indeed has done so in a number of other cases. The reconstructions have usually been prompted by the state of the gardens when taken on by the Trust; in many cases they had either disappeared or were derelict.

Westbury Court, hidden away in Gloucestershire close to the Forest of Dean, is a reconstructed garden of unique historical importance. Created by Maynard Colchester between 1696 and 1705, it is the most complete surviving example in England of a Dutch-inspired water garden, but when the National Trust agreed to take on the property in 1967 it was in an advanced state of decay. After raising sufficient money from a public appeal—assisted by a large anonymous gift—and from a grant from the Historic Buildings Council, the National Trust was able to embark upon restoration. It was greatly helped by the discovery of Maynard Colchester's account books for the years 1696 to 1705. The work entailed dredging, relining and refilling the garden's two canals—one a long rectangle, the other T-shaped—and taking down and rebuilding the delightful gazebo at one end of the rectangular canal. A formal parterre was laid out to one side of the canals, where Kip's view of the garden, engraved in 1717, shows that one originally existed and in one corner of the garden a second pavilion was restored and given its own small walled garden, filled with seventeenth-

The restored canal and completely rebuilt pavilion at Westbury Court.

century plants. The restoration of Westbury is arguably the National Trust's most significant contribution to England's gardening history.

One of the most extensive reconstructions the National Trust has taken on is the landscape garden at Claremont in Surrey. Claremont is of particular interest because it contains the work of John Vanbrugh, who built a house for himself there, and the landscape artists Charles Bridgeman and William Kent. All of their various contributions to the garden were completely overgrown and obscured until the National Trust began, in 1975, the painstaking work of clearance and reconstruction. Now the long view from the bowling green to Vanbrugh's castellated belvedere is open again, Bridgeman's tiered grass amphitheatre has been cleared, its slopes regraded and reseeded, and the lake originally planned by Bridgeman and later extended by Kent has been dredged and Kent's pavilion on an island restored.

Claremont has recently been joined by the other most important landscape garden in Surrey, Painshill Park, originally laid out by its owner, Charles Hamilton, between 1738 and 1773, and now reconstructed by the Painshill Park Trust. The work has included restoring the Temple of Bacchus, with an Adam ceiling and fantastic grotto.

As at both Hatfield and Helmingham, it has often been the quality of the period architecture of a house—not necessarily on the scale of either of these—which has prompted the creation of a garden with an historically sympathetic style and character. This has certainly been the case at Chenies Manor House, in Buckinghamshire, which was bought by Colonel and Mrs MacLeod Matthews during the 1950s. Chenies was built, mostly during the sixteenth century, by the Russell family, Earls and later Dukes of Bedford. The family lived at Chenies until the Civil War when they moved to Woburn Abbey. Chenies was thereafter occupied by a succession of tenants until it was bought by the MacLeod Matthewses who have determined to recreate the gardens around the house as they would have been for the Tudor Russells—when Henry VIII and many members of his court were visitors.

The most direct re-creation is the labyrinth or maze to the north of the house, where the Tudor gardens lay, and which has been reconstructed from a picture at Woburn Abbey dated 1580. In the main part of the new gardens, now to the south and south-west of the house, the formal sunken garden, with narrow beds, retaining walls and flagged paths, is most reminiscent of the one at Hampton Court. There is also a physic garden consisting of neat beds of herbs and a formal garden with yew and box topiary.

The time which marked a sort of eleventh hour for formal gardening in England before the onslaught of the landscape movement was the 1730s. This was when Mawley Hall in Shropshire was built, one of a series of distinctive red-brick houses built in the West Midlands during the early eighteenth century by Francis Smith of Warwick. Later in the century Mawley was duly

143

Claremont. The view across the bowling green to Vanbrugh's castellated belvedere, all restored and recreated by the National Trust.

Part of the formal garden at the Manor House, Chenies.

Fairfield House. An abundance of climbing roses.

Tremeer. The stream along the edge of the garden,
with candelabra primulas in flower.

Helmingham Hall. Looking across the knot garden and formally arranged rose garden to the stable building beyond.

Chenies Manor House. The formal sunken garden, created in a style sympathetic to the period of the house.

surrounded with its own landscape which enhanced the already outstanding views over the Shropshire countryside. In the early 1960s Mr and Mrs Anthony Galliers-Pratt bought the house and sought a way of enhancing its period quality.

Below the west front they have made a pair of matching parterres, enclosed with box and filled with low, mainly silver plants. More intriguing is the large herb garden, where a pattern of rectangular beds contains over 200 varieties of herb. These are enclosed by low brick walls supporting brick paths and while slender columnar junipers line one, a series of stone statues have been placed along another. In this way the Galliers-Pratts have recalled the formality still widespread in gardens at the time of the house's construction, although it was already under siege, and given a contrast to the natural landscape in a manner which is most pleasing and effective. As in the case of other successful re-creations, Mawley is by no means an unimaginative copy of a garden from a past period, but one which sensitively compliments the architecture of a house at the same time as providing much of gardening interest—both historical and horticultural.

10
FROM CREATION TO CONSERVATION

Gardens throughout history have been confronted by a two-fold challenge. First, the initial stages of conception and creation, of planning, laying out and planting. Second, the quest for survival which has never been guaranteed purely by virtue of their existence, as it has for houses. Survival of a garden calls for continuous—or at least regular—attention and maintenance and it is the failure to meet these demands which has often proved responsible for decline and eventual disappearance. In the case of eighteenth-century landscapes, the basic reason why so many have survived, wholly or in part, compared to gardens or landscapes from other periods, is that they have been largely self-maintaining. While their trees have grown to maturity, a long-term process in itself, their broad expanses of grass have been kept neatly cropped by cattle, sheep or deer and the whole scene has steadily grown up over decades in a largely natural manner.

These, however, are the exception. For the majority of gardens the chances of long-term survival have always been uncertain, at times hazardous and never more so than for those made since the war. Now reaching varying stages of maturity they are faced, for one thing, by the pressure of maintenance which, if always a factor, has become increasingly acute with the dramatic rise in costs of both labour and machinery. To take one example, the fact that 95 per cent of the students leaving the Thames Polytechnic School of Landscape will go to institutional rather than private gardens reflects on how self-reliant, in labour terms, most private gardens and their owners have been forced to become.[1]

On the other hand, not only does the expanding popularity of both established and new courses in landscape work, garden design and horticulture point to a burgeoning interest, but in recent years within the reduced market of privately-owned gardens, there are both more people wishing to finish their training and find work there rather than in institutional gardens, and more owners prepared to pay for a well-trained head gardener. Old style head gardeners, born and bred on the estates they would later work on, as generations of their families had before them, and taken into training on leaving school to learn the craft of gardening and plantsmanship as evolved in the gardens of country houses, have steadily declined as the way of life in the country has undergone fundamental changes. The new-style head gardeners have a diploma, if not a degree, quite possibly are not countrymen by birth, but have horticultural knowledge and an enthusiasm for plants and gardens which matches that of their predecessors. The trend towards equality of the sexes has been as marked among gardeners as in any other group of people and today many of the outstanding head gardeners around the country are women.

The self-reliance forced upon owners is an underlying cause of the personalization which has become such a widespread characteristic of gardens. People have gardened for their own enjoyment; what else, after all, justifies the amount of hard work called for. In many cases they have been happy to plan only for their own lifetimes. This in itself has led to the criticism that, since the war, we have become a nation of 'one generation' gardeners. If unfair and historically not a contemporary development, this has gained a new relevance during the age in which we now live. The easy, year-round availability of a limitless array of plants, which never existed in the past, has been brought about principally by the revolution of containerization and the spectacular rise of the 'garden centre'. This advent of what could be called 'fast-plant' gardening, added to the ascendant position which plants have assumed in the minds of many gardeners, to the detriment and at times exclusion of an overall design, has promoted a tendency towards gardens which, if delightful and rewarding in the short term, lack the foundations or structure to give the chance of long-term survival. The fact that the 'hard' features—walls, paths, steps, gateways, pools, etc., which can provide the long-lasting foundations—are often prohibitively expensive is a stark reality of gardening today. But in many cases, it is also the failure to plant trees and hedges because it is felt that they take too long to grow, which unnecessarily robs a garden of a proper framework.

'It is one thing to make a garden to be enjoyed in one's own lifetime and quite another to anticipate change and to provide for its continuous conservation, which is the purpose of the National Trust. Not only does it demand a policy both for the general approach to its style and character and for the details of its planting or upkeep, but it also requires a consistency of purpose that goes beyond individual Head Gardeners or tenants.'[2]

Here John Sales, Gardens Adviser to the National Trust, is talking specifically about the management of National Trust gardens, something of a special case in that they are no longer in private ownership and long-term conservation is one of the Trust's major priorities when taking on any property. None the less, the principles he outlines are applicable to any garden aspiring to a long-term future. In many cases the problem is compounded for gardeners by uncertainty about their successors. For their garden to continue to thrive an essential prerequisite is that their children, or whoever else takes on the property, are actively interested. While the aristocratic patrons of the past were able to build their houses and lay out their gardens in the confidence that they would be occupied and enjoyed by generations of their descendants, this is rarely the case today.

147

Happily, however, new owners have often proved capable of and enthusiastic about maintaining and developing gardens begun by their predecessors. Since John Phillimore left The Postern a few years ago his garden has been conscientiously kept up to a high standard by his successors, Mr and Mrs David Coaten. More ambitious work has been carried out in Sir James Horlick's woodland garden at Achamore House on the Isle of Gigha where the new owner, David Landale—in conjunction with the National Trust for Scotland, to whom Sir James left the formidable collection of plants in his garden—has embarked upon extensive rejuvenation and replanting, made necessary in particular by a number of the hedges, which Sir James had originally planted to form divisions and provide protection, growing far beyond their intended size. At another woodland garden, Tremeer in Cornwall, Major-General Eric Harrison's outstanding collections of camellias and rhododendrons and the rest of his garden are equally well looked after and kept up by Dr Haslam and Mrs Hopwood.

Since the war the National Trust has played a vital role in the conservation of gardens by taking on, maintaining and, in a number of cases, completely restoring gardens of outstanding historical interest and importance. The historical factor is of decisive importance but as yet the Trust's umbrella does not extend to gardens as young as any completely made during the last forty years. In the hope of providing similar security, a number of owners have in recent years established and endowed private charitable trusts which will continue to manage and perpetuate their gardens. Such trusts have been set up at the Garden House, Buckland Monochorum and Rosemoor, both in Devon, Great Comp in Kent, Jenkyn Place in Hampshire and Broadleas in Wiltshire. All five gardens with their established reputations for excellence, are open to the public on a regular basis, the visitors indeed playing an all-important role by providing income to supplement initial endowments.

Determination to preserve individual gardens has been joined increasingly during the last decade by a drive for the conservation of specific plants. Since the war economic pressures have severely threatened and depleted the numbers of traditional nurserymen who could be relied on to maintain stocks of plants, however limited and irregular the demand for them among gardeners. Their outlook was exemplified by Harold Hillier, who once remarked that he liked to have 'ten of everything, to be on the safe side' at his family's world-famous nursery and arboretum in Hampshire. When the *Hilliers Manual of Trees and Shrubs* was first published in 1971 it contained descriptions of some 8,000 trees, shrubs and climbing plants. They were all available. Not only did the oil crisis of the 1970s have a disastrous effect on the price of the fuel needed to heat the acres of greenhouses where plants were propagated and raised, but at the same time nurserymen had to compete—at least in terms of the general, if not the specialist, market—with the advent of the garden centre which by this time was following in the wake of the supermarket and bringing American-style convenience and containerized shopping to the ever expanding gardening public.

It was partly the demise of the traditional nurseryman which aroused concern for individual plants. In 1978 the campaign received its most decisive boost when, after a conference organized under the aegis of the Royal Horticultural Society, the National Council for the Conservation of Plants and Gardens (NCCPG) was established. Now based at the RHS garden at Wisley, the Council is organized in county groups and has an increasing membership of over 4,000. Its initial priority was to outline a general conservation policy, an important part of which was the setting up of national collections of individual plant genera and groups. The owners or curators of each collection aim to grow and, where possible, distribute, as many varieties of each group or genus as they can; and while many of the total of around 350 are held by institutional or botanic gardens, a vital number have been established in private gardens.[3] (National collections are noted in the Gazetteer which forms Part III.)

In 1986 the publication of *The Vanishing Garden* by Christopher Brickell and Fay Sharman highlighted the threat of disappearance that hung over individual plants with descriptions of many hundreds from eighty genera, all of them endangered. While some of the plants have always been rare and grown only by specialists, the book's most important message concerned the plight of numerous plants which were not only common in English gardens in the past, but were traditional plants established in this country for centuries. As the authors concluded in their introduction: 'This book is intended as a stimulant, to encourage interest in our garden plants, old and new, and their continued survival in the future. It is not and never could be a *vademecum* of all cultivated plants in danger, but has been written to draw attention to the grave losses that have already occurred and are still happening now.'[4]

While the 1950s and 1960s witnessed the production of an avalanche of new varieties of plants, not least thousands of garish new modern roses, the conservationist mood of recent years has turned many gardeners towards reviving traditional plants. After being virtually ousted for decades by hybrid teas, floribundas and modern shrub varieties, and more than a little as a result of painstaking research and promotion by Graham Stuart Thomas, old-fashioned shrub roses have once again returned to widespread popularity.

In addition to the revived interest in traditional garden plants, the plight of many British wild flowers as a result of modern farming methods has also brought about concern for their safety. Now those flowers which once thronged the hedgerows, roadsides and pastures all over the country can be found being carefully nurtured in many gardens. At Helmingham Hall in Suffolk, as well as the new formal garden an important addition has been the meadow garden planted beneath the fruit trees of an old orchard beyond the

149

main Elizabethan garden. Here, in summer, the tall grass is filled with drifts of ox-eye daisies. Undoubtedly the best known among such new meadow gardens is the one made by the Prince of Wales at Highgrove in Gloucestershire. At Bradenham Hall in Norfolk, cowslips have been successfully encouraged to naturalize among the established throngs of daffodils beneath the trees of the arboretum.

If conservationist worries have aroused concern for and general interest in growing traditional plants their use in gardens today is in harmony with the philosophy of contemporary gardeners. The smaller scale—in many cases compulsory—and the intimacy of enclosures idealized by Sissinghurst combines with an assumption that a garden should be primarily a place of natural beauty. The cottage garden dream, harking back to the past in a most appealing manner and conjuring up wistful but potent images, has been transported into gardens of all shapes and sizes and, most widely, into country gardens. In a decisive manner it has both perpetuated the traditions and principles established by William Robinson and Gertrude Jekyll, and of the Arts and Crafts movement of their time, as well as adapting them for contemporary gardens.

Among other things it has reiterated what has been true throughout history—that for the great majority of English people a garden is a place for growing things, while ornament and architecture play a subsidiary role. It is a place in the country, harmonious with nature and controlled more by the turn of the seasons than by any human influence. This, beyond anything else, has ensured that modernist or abstract influences have been minimal in Britain compared with, for instance, Scandinavia or the United States. The conception of a garden as an adjunct of the house, an 'exterior living room' may be perhaps suitable for a tiny London garden, but for the average English country garden it is impractical because of the weather for most of the year. Nor is it sufficiently interesting. A paved patio, with designer furniture, terracotta pots, french doors into the house and a pool nearby, does not compare for most English people with a well-stocked border or bank of shrubs in full flower.

There is no doubt that since the Second World War people have become conscious, as they never were in the past, that in their gardens they are continuing long-established, important and delightful traditions. This in itself has engendered immense enthusiasm and activity. It has combined with the appreciation of gardens, and of making a garden, as an antidote to so much of the stress of contemporary life to bring about an unprecedented upsurge over the last forty years which will unquestionably continue into the future. Thus, while many gardens will come and go and enjoy sadly short lives, new ones will constantly be appearing to take their place, to provide new interest, and to conserve and enhance the rich and venerable traditions of British gardens.

PART III
GAZETTEER

GAZETTEER

Note: The names given with each entry are the owners at the time of writing. Where the garden was originally made by a previous owner this is noted. Page references refer to more detailed descriptions in the preceding chapters.

It is impossible to give accurate details of opening to the public as these change every year. All that is mentioned is where a garden is open occasionally or regularly. Where no mention is made the garden is not open. The majority of gardens open for the National Gardens Scheme and details can be found in their annual guide, *Gardens of England and Wales Open to the Public*, the 'Yellow Book'. Details of gardens open more regularly can be found in the annual *Historic Houses, Castles and Gardens in Great Britain and Ireland*. The National Gardens Scheme is abbreviated to NGS, the Historic Houses, Castles and Gardens guide to HHCG.

Abbots Ripton Hall, Huntingdon
The Lord and Lady de Ramsey

Abbots Ripton has extensive gardens where quality of plants and design is complemented by architectural features and buildings in various styles, designed by Peter Foster. Lord de Ramsey was assisted with parts of the design by Humphrey Waterfield. The garden has been built up around an existing framework of lawns and outstanding mature trees and the water of the Abbots Ripton brook flows through. Ambitious formal features such as the double herbaceous borders and grey border contrast with shrubberies planted with unusual specimens. In one direction the design is extended into the landscape beyond by a new five-acre lake. Throughout the gardens manage to combine a feeling of immaculate orderliness with continual surprise to an unusual degree. *See pages 97–101.*

Garden open occasionally for NGS.

Achamore House, Isle of Gigha
Mr David Landale and the National Trust for Scotland

Unquestionably one of the most absorbing and individual of all the west coast of Scotland gardens, created by Colonel Sir James Horlick after he bought the Isle of Gigha in 1944. His woodland garden was brilliantly devised leading between small open glades and areas of constantly varied planting. As well as these enclosed areas there are a number of theatrical flourishes, such as the main vista up the drive towards the house. Rhododendrons were Sir James's first love and the gardens contain many rare and unusual varieties, especially tender ones which thrive in Gigha's mild, if windswept climate. Similarly there are numerous other trees and shrubs ideally suited to the conditions. Since Sir James's death in 1972, and the subsequent purchase of the island by David Landale, much necessary clearance and replanting has been carried out to revive certain areas. *See pages 112–14.*

Garden open regularly.

Badminton House, Gloucestershire
The Duke and Duchess of Beaufort

Since moving to Badminton House in 1984, when he inherited the dukedom from his cousin, the Duke and Duchess have embarked on creating extensive gardens on the east and south sides of the house. The Duchess had already made the delightful garden at their previous home, the Cottage, Badminton, with the help of Russell Page (*see page 53*). Although Badminton is surrounded by its enormous park, originally laid out by Henry Somerset, Duke of Beaufort, during the 1680s and added to during the eighteenth century by Thomas Wright, as well as being embellished by the series of buildings designed by William Kent, there was little real garden when the Duke and Duchess moved to the house. Advised again by Russell Page, until his death in 1985 and subsequently by François Goffinet, she has planned a formal style of garden with box edging and hornbeam hedges enclosing herbaceous borders, a silver and white border, a shrub rose garden and many other planting features, all providing a new and suitable area of unity between the house and its park.

Barnsley House, Gloucestershire
Mrs David Verey

Barnsley has achieved a widespread reputation in recent years, both in England and the United States. The garden has been created by Rosemary Verey, who is also widely known for her garden books, and her late husband David, the architectural historian. It combines a variety of features and a balance of formality and informality, the first generally in the design and architectural features, the second in the details of much of the planting, which has become since the Second World War a hallmark of gardens of quality. Like many of its contemporaries it is relatively small, covering only three and a half acres. The interest and ingenuity achieved within such a limited area lies at the heart of the garden's appeal. *See pages 74–8.*

Garden open regularly (see NGS and HHCG).

Biddick Hall, County Durham
Lord Lambton

Italian-inspired formal gardens of outstanding quality as unexpected in the industrial north-east of England as the classical red-brick house. The gardens were laid out by Lord Lambton in the 1950s and 1960s as a progression from the house to the distant point where the garden merges with the park around Lambton Castle which lies beyond. There is a geometric structure of hedges, superb urns and statues and an overall impression of studied composition, as well as

delightful touches such as the apiary garden with chinoiserie beehives. A firmness and yet fluidity of structure rarely seen in English gardens made since 1945. *See pages 192–4.*

Bradenham Hall, East Dereham, Norfolk
Colonel and Mrs Richard Allhusen

An extensive garden planned on an ambitious scale since the 1950s, which combines formal design in some areas with an impressive array of plants. One of the great features is the springtime array of daffodils planted in tens of thousands around the trees of the arboretum on either side of the drive. Trees are of major importance and the arboretum now contains nearly one thousand different varieties. Elsewhere a series of yew hedges surround geometric enclosures containing a variety of features such as an herbaceous border, rose garden and pleached lime walk. The garden's immaculate appearance proves that large gardens do not have to be labour-intensive, as Colonel and Mrs Allhusen manage it themselves with one gardener, his wife and one other part-time. *See pages 69–72.*

Broadleas, Devizes, Wiltshire
Lady Anne Cowdray and Broadleas
   Gardens Ltd.

Conventional areas of garden around the house have been greatly enhanced by numerous unusual plants added by Lady Anne. Her main achievement is the woodland garden, made in a natural and sheltered coombe. Here an impressive variety of ornamental and flowering trees and shrubs as well as spring bulbs, including a number of rare and surprisingly tender varieties, have been planted informally among native standard oaks and Scots pines in a manner characteristic of modern woodland gardens. The garden contains the NCCPG National Collection of Euonymus, excepting the *fortunei* and *japonicus* cultivars. It has recently become a private charitable trust. *See pages 117–19.*

Gardens open regularly (see NGS).

Brook Cottage, Alkerton, Oxfordshire
Mr and Mrs David Hodges

An adventurous modern garden of four acres made on a largely featureless west-facing slope of rough grazing land. Clever plant associations and design—Mr Hodges is an architect—with the ground levelled into terraces close to the house and the addition of firm, structural walls, gateways and yew and copper-beech hedges. Existing water has been capitalized upon to make a pond garden for aquatic plants and, at the bottom of the slope in front of the house, a small lake. There are many climbers and foliage plants and unusual specimens in sheltered borders. Towards its perimeters the garden merges into surrounding countryside with a more open style of trees, shrubs and spring bulbs. *See pages 86–8.*

Garden open occasionally for NGS and regularly by appointment.

Burford House, Tenbury Wells, Shropshire
Mr John Treasure

An immaculately maintained garden made by Mr Treasure around the impressive Georgian house since 1954, when he bought the property. Lack of any existing garden, except for a variety of mature trees, gave him the freedom to embark on an impressive modern design and to employ his considerable plantsmanship. Much of the design has easy curving lines; broad sweeps of lawn between large island beds and an informal water garden along the banks of a stream. Elsewhere there are more formal pools, terraces, flights of steps and decorative urns and vases. Among the quantity of annuals, herbaceous plants, trees and shrubs with which Mr Treasure has populated the garden, is the almost comprehensive collection of clematis for which the garden is renowned. Next door is the famous Treasure of Tenbury clematis nursery, which holds the NCCPG National Collection of Clematis. In addition there is a clematis museum in the old stable block containing an exhibition on the history of clematis.

Garden open regularly.

Chenies Manor House, Buckinghamshire
Lieutenant-Colonel and Mrs Macleod
 Matthews

Gardens recreated in a style harmonious with the Tudor house, once home of the Dukes of Bedford and scene of Henry VIII's wife Katherine Howard's adultery with Thomas Culpepper. A small 'labyrinth' has been reconstructed from a drawing dated 1580 at the Bedfords' seat Woburn Abbey. There is a rectangular sunken garden, similar to the one at Hampton Court, with narrow terraces of lawn and flower-beds and low retaining walls descending to a central lawn. Elsewhere there is a physic garden, filled with herbs, a formal garden with yew and box topiary and a white garden planned by the garden designer, James Garnock. *See pages 143–4.*

Garden open regularly (see HHCG).

Chilcomb House, Dorset
Mr and Mrs John Hubbard

A delightful garden made since 1969, totally in keeping with the farmhouse's character and the deeply rural surroundings. Only two acres in size, John and Caryl Hubbard's creation is an exemplary illustration of the small scale and intimacy which have become such widespread features of post-war gardens. The exuberance of planting is tempered by pastel colours and neat design. Flowers and shrubs blend happily with fruit and vegetables and there are particularly good old-fashioned and climbing roses and clematis, as well as many traditional herbaceous plants. *See pages 82–4.*

Garden open occasionally (see NGS).

Cholmondeley Castle, Cheshire
The Marquess and Marchioness of
 Cholmondeley

Since 1950 Lord and Lady Cholmondeley have carried out considerable re-creation and extension of the gardens with the parkland setting which is contemporary with the romantic Regency castle. In the Temple garden they restored the rockery and waterfall with the help of Mr McKenna, expanded the stream into a lake and added a second temple—a rotunda with a wrought-iron dome. In planning and planting the large area of the Glade the Cholmondeleys were assisted by James Russell and the area is now filled with many flowering and ornamental trees and shrubs. To one side herbaceous borders lead to the rose garden, where a series of raised beds edged with stone and lavender contain shrub and climbing roses. Lady Cholmondeley has completely replanted the terrace immediately below the south and east fronts of the castle and a new cherry walk leads away into the park from the far end of the east terrace. It has been an ambitious project and the gardens are on a scale which has become unusual since the war. *See pages 56–7.*

Garden open regularly (see HHCG).

Clapton Court, Crewkerne, Somerset
Captain and Mrs Simon Loder

Clapton has two distinct garden areas and styles: to one side of the house conventional terraces, lawns, a formal rose garden and other borders, which were originally the work of the Loders' predecessor, Louis Martineau, and the woodland garden in another direction from the house which is primarily the Loders' creation. Martineau lived at Clapton from 1950 to 1978, when the Loders came. They have left the framework of the formal areas constructed by Martineau virtually unchanged, but altered and added to much of the planting. As they have steadily added new plants in the woodland garden they have been careful to retain the overall atmosphere of natural woodland. The formal areas are now cleverly linked to the woodland by an intermediate area of open planting along a stream.

Garden open regularly (see NGS and HHCG).

Claremont, Surrey
The National Trust

Claremont is one of the most ambitious and successful restorations carried out by the National Trust—or anyone else—since the Second World War. The work won the Europa Nostra Diploma of Merit in 1980. Virtually all the features of the eighteenth-century landscape, jointly the work of Vanbrugh, Bridgeman and Kent, were obscured or overgrown when the restoration was begun in 1975. The major success was the uncovering of Bridgeman's amphitheatre from beneath a jungle of laurels, rhododendrons and fully-grown cedars, and subsequent regrassing of the curving terraces. The amphitheatre is unique. *See pages 143–4.*

Garden open regularly (see NGS and HHCG).

Coates Manor, Fittleworth, Sussex
Mrs G.H. Thorp

Mrs Thorp's experience as a flower-arranger is clearly evident from the plants she grows whose outstanding feature is subtle association of tree and shrub foliage. When she bought the small Elizabethan manor house in 1960 the present garden was mostly covered with derelict pig-sties. The restrained choice of plants throughout disguises the garden's small size of only one acre, enabling it to be full of interest throughout the year without the appearance of overcrowding. A brick wall extending across the garden from the house supports a number of climbers and provides an important backbone to the structure. Ornamental trees are a feature of the garden, as are the many different varieties of cornus. Mrs Thorp has successfully shown how even such a small garden can be outward-looking into the surrounding countryside by breaking the long protective cypress hedge, which forms the boundary on one side, with a low brick clairvoyée a few yards wide, allowing extensive views out. Thoughtful planning has made the most of a limited area at the same time as keeping maintenance requirements minimal in an exemplary manner.

Garden open occasionally (see NGS).

Coniston Cold, Skipton, Yorkshire
Mr and Mrs Michael Bannister

The garden has been made around an elegant neo-Georgian house built by the Bannisters in 1972 and designed by Neville MacKay. Lanning Roper assisted with the planting and landscaping, the latter involving most successful clearing and grassing of the slope in front of the house opening up superb views across the twenty-four-acre lake, dug in 1846, and surrounding parkland and woods planted towards the end of the nineteenth century. Some of the new borders cleverly follow the outline of the much larger nineteenth-century house which was replaced. The impressive fluted Doric columns and their entablature from the old portico have been retained, free-standing, as a feature of the garden. The Bannisters are now extending planting into the woodland behind the house. *See pages 57–8.*

Dalton Hall, Westmorland
Mr and Mrs Anthony Mason-Hornby

Dalton Hall was the last house to be designed

and built by Sir Clough Williams-Ellis. It is one of his best works. As with many of his other commissions, he planned the lay-out of the immediate surroundings, including garden ornaments and the general details of planting. At Dalton this included the fore-court between the entrance front of the house and the old stable building, the horseshoe-shaped garden on the far side of the house, and the siting and building of the temple which re-uses the pillars from a portico of the old, demolished house. Both house and garden were linked to the fine parkland with which Dalton is blessed, with characteristic ease by Sir Clough Williams-Ellis. *See pages 109–10.*

Denmans, Fontwell, Sussex
Mrs J.H. Robinson and John Brookes

A most individual, modern plantsman's garden of three acres, made predominantly during the last thirty years by Mrs Robinson. Since establishing his school of garden design at the Clock House on one side of the garden, John Brookes has been closely involved with the design and planting of many areas. After the death of her husband Mrs Robinson began transforming what had been a com-mercial market garden. Given the advanta-geous position close to the South Coast the garden is full of unusual plants, either partially tender or sun-loving. The garden is intrinsically modern in that Mrs Robinson has used plants architecturally, and in great pro-fusion, grouping them to create different combined effects and endeavouring to pro-vide the garden with year-round interest. Plants are allowed to seed themselves freely throughout the garden. At the same time gravel is used extensively as an alternative material to grass, partly for its low main-tenance requirements. Most effective is the dry stream course of pebbles and gravel, which winds through part of the garden. Where grass is used it is mown to different lengths to emphasize the flowing contours and curves which characterize the garden's design. Among other parts, John Brookes has designed and planted the area around a pond and the informal herb garden in the walled garden. *See page 55.*

Garden open regularly (see NGS and HHCG).

The Dower House, Boughton,
  Northamptonshire
Lady Scott

The Dower House is a plantsman's garden of the highest quality, begun by the late Sir David Scott and his first wife, but most sub-stantially a partnership between him and his second wife, Valerie Finnis. It is divided into three areas; the first immediately in front of the house, the second in the walled garden where the main feature is a series of raised beds containing thousands of alpines and other small plants—Lady Scott's forte—and the third an adjoining area of around one hundred island beds divided by flowing grass paths, each with its own name, character and grouping of plants and all devised by Sir David. For a small site of two acres the wealth of plants is second to none. *See pages 121–4.*

Garden open occasionally (see NGS) and by appointment.

Dundonnell House, Ross and Cromarty
Alan and Neil Roger

An intriguing garden, situated on the remote, extreme west coast of Scotland just south of Ullapool. Since acquiring Dundonnell in 1956 the Rogers have transformed what was a traditional Scottish walled garden on one side of the charming eighteenth-century house, into something quite unexpected in this part of the country. Retaining the long-established geometric pattern of narrow paths, Alan Roger, a knowledgeable and adventurous gardener, has radically altered the planting. Features include an informal herb garden, ingeniously enclosed by slatted screens sup-porting climbers, a laburnum tunnel, an extensive collection of bonsai and two large mixed borders. For variety there are aviaries containing exotic birds, and peacocks wandering freely.

Garden open occasionally (see Scotland's Garden Scheme guide).

Everton Park, Sandy, Bedfordshire
The Lord and Lady Pym

Everton Park is primarily of interest because the garden was designed by Geoffrey Jellicoe. The neo-Georgian house was built 1968–9, on the edge of the large park laid out by

Humphry Repton round Lord Pym's family home, Hasells Hall. Everton Park and its garden are positioned on a dramatic escarpment beyond which, to the west, the land falls away to the Bedfordshire plain, affording spectacular views over the countryside. Jellicoe's great success was in planning the garden to take full advantage of the surroundings without being overpowered by their scale, at the same time as providing the necessary privacy required by his client. There are two main vistas: one from the study window of the house across Repton's park to a cedar tree standing beside the old house, the other past the end of the beech hedge, planted along the front of the garden to block out new developments at Sandy in the distance, across the plain below dissected by the main King's Cross to Edinburgh railway line—a piece of modern landscape that would undoubtedly have appealed to Jellicoe. The planting is designed to bring the garden to a peak during the parliamentary recess in August and September, when the Pyms spend longest at Everton. As with many other gardens designed by Jellicoe, the detailed plans of the planting were drawn up by his wife Susan.

Fairfield House, Hambledon, Hampshire
Mr and Mrs Peter Wake

Since Mr and Mrs Wake bought Fairfield House in 1970, the garden has been designed to enable them to maintain the four acres themselves with occasional help. Fairfield is the garden for a compulsive enthusiast for old-fashioned shrub and climbing roses—of which there is an extensive collection. A number of the shrub and specie roses are grown free-standing as individuals, mixing in an informal orchard setting with ornamental and flowering trees. The enclosing brick walls are extensively clothed in climbing varieties. Mature cedars, limes and beech shelter the approach to the Regency house and the ground beneath them has now been extensively planted with spring bulbs.
See pages 131–3.

Garden open occasionally (see NGS) and by appointment.

The Garden House, Buckland Monochorum, Devon
The Fortescue Garden Trust

Lionel Fortescue was an expert and highly critical plantsman and the garden he created between 1945 and his death in 1981 continues to reflect these qualities. The eight acres, much of which form a series of terraces descending from the house to the old walled garden, provide the setting for a constantly varied array of plants—all of them first-class specimens, as he only tolerated the best. Flowering trees, such as magnolias, rhododendrons—of which Fortescue bred many outstanding hybrids—unusual shrubs, herbaceous perennials and spring bulbs have been over the years assiduously grouped and arranged so as to show off their individual qualities to best advantage at the same time as giving a satisfying overall picture. The high standards have been continued by the recently created charitable trust and the garden has justifiably built up an important reputation. *See pages 124–6.*

Garden open regularly (see NGS and HHCG).

Garmelow Manor, Eccleshall, Staffordshire
Mr and Mrs Arnold Machin

The distinguished sculptor, Arnold Machin, had already created a garden of great interest at nearby Offley Rock before he came to live at Garmelow in 1979. Since then he has created a garden of considerable individuality which clearly reflects his professional skills and interests. The setting for part of the garden is a series of striking farm buildings, which Machin has incorporated into the design in an unusually sympathetic manner. The other main area is around an existing lake where he has himself constructed a number of architectural features near the lakeside: a boat-house, summer-house and cascade over a grotto, a brick screen with open Gothic arches and, on the far side of the lake, a temple designed by his son Francis. *See pages 84–5.*

Glazenwood, Braintree, Essex
Mr and Mrs D. Baer

Glazenwood is a place of considerable historical interest, in that between 1821 and 1852 it was the home of Samuel Curtis, founder of the Botanical Magazine and author of a number of distinguished horticultural books, including *A Monograph of the Genus Camellia*. It was saved from dereliction by the Baers who bought it in 1964. At that time a ginkgo planted by Curtis had appeared through the roof of the house and in the main area of garden hothouses, which had once supplied soft fruits to the Cunard liners, were in a state of total decay. The Baers' work has been impressive. The hot-houses and the system of underground pipes which fed them were swept away and replaced by a large lawn, with a long shrub border on one side and trees supporting climbing roses fronting the surrounding woodland along two others. Only the peach packing-house was retained, to become a summer-house for a swimming pool, around which are borders of old-fashioned shrub roses, and beyond the woodland garden containing one or two of Curtis's original pear trees. On another side of the house old rose beds were replaced by a croquet lawn. As well as retaining the connection with Curtis, and re-creating and rationalizing the seven acres so that they are able to maintain it with one full-time gardener, the Baers have created a garden of considerable interest.

Garden open occasionally (see NGS).

Great Comp, Borough Green, Kent
The Great Comp Charitable Trust

A remarkable garden made during the last thirty years and for much of that time maintained without help by Mr and Mrs Cameron who have recently created a charitable trust to look after Great Comp into the future. The seven acres contain an enormous quantity of plants, ranging from lofty conifers to low perennial ground-cover, and have grown up in a strikingly contemporary style, with grass paths winding informally between bold groups of dense planting, together giving a woodland effect in many areas. The garden is dissected by two vistas opening out from the two main fronts of the house, close to which more conventional lawns, terraces and borders extend the garden's range of design and plant material. Along its network of paths Great Comp presents many unusual specimens, particularly flowering trees and shrubs as well as the surprise of occasional architectural features. *See pages 116–17.*

Garden open regularly (see NGS and HHCG).

Ham House, Surrey
The National Trust

When the National Trust acquired Ham House from the Tollemache family in 1948 the formal gardens that had once surrounded the Duke and Duchess of Lauderdale's great house had virtually disappeared. Since 1976 the National Trust has carried out a programme of re-creation to an extremely high standard, restoring to the house a setting totally harmonious with its appearance and lavish interiors. *See pages 140–1.*

Garden open regularly (see HHCG).

Hardwick Hall, Derbyshire
The National Trust

As well as restoring the existing gardens at Hardwick, the National Trust, which took on the property in 1959 after it was offered to the Treasury in lieu of death duties by the Duke of Devonshire, has added one of the largest herb gardens in the country. This was added during the 1970s to be in keeping with the Elizabethan house and fills one quarter of the enormous walled garden. Interest is added to the herb garden by the labelling giving the culinary and medicinal uses of the plants.

Garden open regularly (see NGS and HHCG).

Haseley Court, Little Haseley, Oxfordshire
Mr and Mrs Desmond Heyward and Mrs C.G. Lancaster

It is perhaps not surprising that someone who made such an impact on post-war English country-house interior design as Nancy Lancaster, should have enjoyed a comparable, if far more private, success when she embarked upon creating a garden. In its heyday in the late 1960s and 1970s her garden at Haseley Court seemed to those people who knew it to contain many of the features and characteristics which are most satisfying in a country-house garden. When she bought the house there was already the nineteenth-century topiary garden on one side. Mrs Lancaster commissioned Geoffrey Jellicoe to lay out a broad terrace along the main front of the house overlooking the entrance forecourt. Her main gardening efforts were concentrated in the large rectangular area, walled on two sides and originally the kitchen garden, but by the 1950s nothing better than a field. The other two sides were enclosed by gravel paths beneath tunnels of hornbeam. Mrs Lancaster divided the central area into four, each with its own style and character, and planted deep borders beneath the perimeter walls. The overall effect was one of ingenuity and variety, a happy mixture of formality and informality between the box edging, paths and lawns, and the mixed, effusive planting. Elsewhere in the gardens an ancient fish-pond was altered to make a formal canal and a spring garden made beneath tall beech trees. Mrs Lancaster has subsequently moved to the Coach House next to Haseley Court, where Mr and Mrs Heyward now live. *See pages 79–80.*

Garden open occasionally (see NGS).

Hatfield House, Hertfordshire
The Marquess and Marchioness of Salisbury

Different parts of the extensive gardens at Hatfield date from different periods in the house's long and distinguished history. In recent years many areas have undergone dramatic change at the hands of the present Marchioness of Salisbury who has carried out a most successful and ambitious re-creation. Her aim has been to redesign and replant the gardens so as to recall the Tudor period of the remaining wing of the old royal palace of Hatfield and the early Stuart origins of the main house itself. The work reveals both considerable skill in the planning and extensive knowledge of the garden styles and plants used during the sixteenth and seventeenth centuries. The intimacy of a Tudor knot garden and small maze contrasts with the formal grandeur of the east garden where, beneath balustraded terraces, large box-edged squares of planting are flanked by rows of clipped ilex trees. *See pages 136–8.*

Garden open regularly (see HHCG).

Hazelby House, Newbury, Berkshire
Mr and Mrs Martin Lane Fox

Created since 1974 from an almost completely empty and derelict site, save for the surviving walls of the old kitchen garden in one area, the garden at Hazelby has an overall conception which few people have rivalled during the last fifteen years. The garden's quality is confirmed by the manner in which the details of design and planting match the vigour of the initial scheme. Classical order and symmetry in the design allow for the romantic nature of the planting; a firm structure of paths, clipped hedges, retaining walls and enclosures around beds and borders filled mainly with mixed shrubs, old-fashioned roses and herbaceous perennials. The house itself is integrated by climbers on the walls, a new orangery on one side and the terrace on another where paving stones alternate with low planting. In contrast to the seclusion of some areas other parts of the garden look outward into the surrounding countryside in true landscape tradition. *See pages 102–7.*

Garden open occasionally (see NGS).

Heaselands, Haywards Heath, Sussex
Mrs Ernest Kleinwort

Heaselands reveals an intriguing combination of pre-war and post-war garden styles on an unusually expansive scale. Broadly speaking the formally planned areas around the house —which was completely rebuilt by Ernest Kleinwort in 1933–4, and now presents a deceptively authentic example of the Sussex manor house style—were laid out before the war. In particular the sunken garden and rock garden are immediately characteristic of country-house gardens of the 1930s. After the war Ernest Kleinwort, whose father had started the Heaselands estate in 1898, and who was himself chairman of the family's merchant bank before his death in 1977, steadily extended the garden into the long valley containing a stream and series of ponds and the woodland beyond. Collections of hybrid rhododendrons and azaleas are outstanding in the woodland garden and the whole twenty acres is maintained to a standard reminiscent of pre-war days.

Garden open occasionally (see NGS).

Helmingham Hall, Stowmarket, Suffolk
The Lord and Lady Tollemache

There have always been gardens to the south of the house at Helmingham, but since 1982 Lord and Lady Tollemache have created a new Elizabethan garden immediately to the north which compliments the architecture of the sixteenth-century house. They were assisted in the design by Lady Salisbury.

Within a rectangular plan formal knot and herb gardens—the former incorporating Lord and Lady Tollemache's initials and the family crest—lead to the rose garden where old-fashioned and specie shrub roses are arranged by family in a simple pattern of large beds. Although only a few years old the overall picture of the garden is already delightful. *See pages 138–40.*

Hillbarn House, Great Bedwyn, Wiltshire
Mr and Mrs A.J. Buchanan

A garden of two acres developed since the 1950s by three successive owners and revealing outstandingly successful continuity. The garden was partly designed by Lanning Roper and is most interesting for its different formal features, small parterre, hornbeam tunnel and arbour, split hornbeam hedge, espalier pear walk, chessboard herb garden and vegetable potager. In addition there are deep borders planned by Lanning Roper and a small garden on one side of the house enclosed by pleached limes. *See pages 58–9.*

Garden open occasionally (see NGS).

Hinton Ampner House, Hampshire
The National Trust

The house and garden of Hinton Ampner are one of the most singular post-war achievements, the work of Ralph Dutton, eighth Lord Sherborne, who left the property to the National Trust on his death in 1985. His work on the house is described in *The Latest Country Houses* by John Martin Robinson. In the extensive garden he effected a complete transformation of the basic framework of terraces to the south of the house, in particular fusing them with the surrounding parkland in a theatrical manner. With a series of views opened up, there appears to be no break between garden and park, lawns seemingly flowing into the pastures beyond. The formality of the terraces, in particular the long walk flanked in one direction by rows of columnar yews, is balanced by other areas of the garden where paths wind between closely planted shrubberies and in the dell. Below the east front of the house is a formal canal garden. Statues, urns and a classical temple enhance the garden's appearance, as does Ralph Dutton's extensive planting, especially of flowering shrubs and trees.

Garden open regularly (see NGS and HHCG).

Horsted Place, Uckfield, Sussex
Horsted Place Country House Hotel

The garden at Horsted was redesigned by Lord and Lady Rupert Nevill after they moved to the house in 1965, with the help of Geoffrey Jellicoe. Jellicoe suggested the series of wrought-iron baskets containing roses and pansies, set in the main lawn, which were copied from a design by Repton for the Brighton Pavilion. Along one side of the lawn Jellicoe planted pleached limes, found in many of his designs, with windows cut in their foliage to give views out to the surrounding parkland. Beyond the lawn, paths lead off between flowering and scented trees and shrubs, one into woodland to the hidden round garden where a circular lawn is enclosed by thick shrubberies and shaded by tall beech trees. Lady Rupert sold Horsted following her husband's death in 1982.

House of Pitmuies, Forfar, Angus
Mrs Farquhar Ogilvie

After coming to the House of Pitmuies in 1966 Mrs Ogilvie and her late husband expanded and redeveloped the garden, building on the preliminary restoration done by his parents after they bought the property in 1945. Skilful design is now matched by varied planting for different times of the year. The south side of the house is brought into the garden by clematis on the walls and the octagonal conservatory at one end. In front is the main area of formal planting: pairs of double herbaceous borders on either side of a rose garden. In one pair of borders the colours are blue and white with silver foliage plants. The others are mixed and backed by hedges of purple prunus. Between these two the central path is aligned with a gateway into the walled garden where, as well as fruit and vegetables, Mrs Ogilvie has added a herb garden. In between the borders the rose garden is planted with predominantly old-fashioned varieties, around a central lily pool and fountain enclosed by paving. Beyond these areas, which attain a peak in late summer, are more informal areas of riverside walks filled with bulbs in the spring and, in particular, an alpine meadow, covered with naturalized miniature crocus, aconites and snowdrops. Elsewhere there are deep shrub borders, carefully positioned new ornamental trees, and primulas and meconopsis in a damp piece of woodland.

Garden open regularly (see Scotland's Garden Scheme guide).

Ince Castle, Saltash, Cornwall
Patricia Viscountess Boyd of Merton

Lord and Lady Boyd originally bought Ince for its seclusion and the opportunity it offered for sailing. From 1960 until Lord Boyd's death in 1983 they created a garden which is now renowned in this most élitist of gardening counties and which Lady Boyd continues to develop. The castle's position on a promontory and spectacular views over the Lynher estuary are used to the full, particularly to the south where a succession of generous terraces drop gently between borders to a formal garden divided by brick and cobble paths. A long shrub border curves up to the east front of the castle, beside the sweep of open lawn on this side—the foreground to views over the water. An extensive woodland garden, filled with the flowering plants for which Cornwall is best known, has been made by steady clearance of undergrowth and planting, around a large central glade with cowslips naturalized in the long grass. Lady Boyd has also made a white garden and a summer garden of 'hot' plants. In spring the straight drive which approaches between hedges is lined for hundreds of yards on either side with carpets of daffodils. *See pages 101–2.*

Garden open occasionally (see NGS).

Jenkyn Place, Bentley, Hampshire
The Jenkyn Place Garden Trust

Jenkyn Place is one of the most extensive gardens to have been made since the war in the Hidcote tradition. A series of different enclosures and areas lead from one to another, and present a steadily unveiling picture. On this basis Major and Mrs Gerald Coke have expanded the garden since 1945, adding new features and plants and broadening the garden's diversity at the same time as strengthening the overall plan. Some of the more architectural features were designed by Trenwith Wills, who also made alterations to the house. Otherwise the work is the Cokes' alone. Attractive existing buildings have been incorporated and evocatively clothed with climbers while wrought-iron gates, brick steps and paths and other statues and ornaments add firmness to the design. In the different parts of the garden there is a wide cross-section of plants which, to some extent, has become a hallmark of gardens of similar calibre. *See pages 66–8.*

Garden open regularly (see NGS and HHCG).

Knightshayes Court, Tiverton, Devon
Lady Amory and the National Trust

When Sir John and Lady Amory came to Knightshayes the garden mainly consisted of uninteresting borders and flower-beds on the Victorian terraces immediately to the south and east of the striking house, built by William Burges for Sir John's grandfather in the 1870s. Having modified and greatly improved these, for instance removing the rose beds which distracted from the sweeping view over the park that drops away southwards to the River Exe, they turned their attention to what was to be their *tour de force*, the woodland garden to the east. The Garden in the Wood, as it has always been called, gradually expanded and now covers nearly twenty acres. Retaining the best specimens of mature trees, the Amorys cleared wide open glades and made winding paths among hosts of new plants—from erythroniums to Asiatic tree magnolias. Beyond the original area of the Garden in the Wood lie Sir John's Wood, Michael's Wood —named after Michael Hickson the head gardener—and No Man's Land, the area in between them. Knightshayes is in the tradition of the woodland gardens established earlier in the twentieth century.
See pages 114–16.

Garden open regularly (see NGS and HHCG).

Langley Grange, Loddon, Norfolk

The main success of the garden at Langley Grange has been to retain the appearance and atmosphere of a farmhouse and its neighbouring buildings at the same time as considerably enhancing their surroundings. A large and highly successful extension to the house looks on to the most ambitious area, a sunken garden enclosed by pleached limes, beyond which a grass path leads between double borders eventually to the focal point of a stone urn set in the woodland beyond. Elsewhere the garden has more flowing lines between shrub borders, island beds and lawn.

Little Moreton Hall, Congleton, Cheshire
The National Trust

When the National Trust took on Little Moreton Hall, originally a moated hall house and expanded in the sixteenth century into the present extraordinary black-and-white timbered house, there was no record of a garden. Since 1972 it has added a knot garden in keeping with the period of the house, with hedges of yew enclosing a square pattern of lawn, low tightly clipped hedges and beds of gravel, with surrounding borders filled mainly with herbs or long-established traditional plants. It is a good example of how the National Trust has not only restored but in some cases added the new dimension of a garden to a number of its properties.

Garden open regularly (see HHCG).

Maenan Hall, Llanrwst, Gwynedd
The Hon. Christopher and Mrs McLaren

The garden at Maenan has been made since 1956, first by Christabel, Lady Aberconway and subsequently by her son, the present owner. Prior to moving to Maenan Lady Aberconway lived at Bodnant, with her husband, the second Lord Aberconway. Not surprisingly, parts of the Maenan garden are in the Bodnant tradition. It is also situated overlooking the Conwy valley and enjoys comparable views to Snowdonia. Among the formal features are a terrace and lawn enclosed by yew hedges in front of the Queen Anne house, with stone sphinxes at the far end. Beyond, a flight of stone steps leads to an avenue of magnolias and cherries and, at the end of one of the main yew hedges, an avenue of standard laburnums, providing subtle variety to the famous laburnum tunnel at Bodnant. Behind the house the walled garden has been planted with flowering trees and roses. Most reminiscent of Bodnant is the atmosphere of

the woodland dell, where the natural terrain of cliffs and streams and background of mature forest trees provide the setting for rhododendrons, azaleas, camellias and many other varieties suited to the woodland conditions. Since 1980 the dell has been continued across the road leading to the house to a new area called the glade. *See pages 118–19.*

Garden open occasionally (see NGS).

Manderston, Duns, Berwickshire
Mr and Mrs Adrian Palmer

The house at Manderston and the gardens which form its more immediate surroundings are one of the great Edwardian essays into architecture and garden making: the former emulating Kedleston in Derbyshire, childhood home of the young wife of James Miller, owner of Manderston at the time, the latter an expansive display of terraces, rose parterres, huge borders and lines of glasshouses, complete with wide gates—some gilded, others set in a classical portico—and plentiful statues and other ornaments. Very different is the woodland garden called the Pheasantry, made from 1957 by Major Bailie, the present owner's grandfather. The Pheasantry lies on the far side of the large lake beneath the south terraces in front of the house. Initially the planting was mainly hybrid and specie rhododendrons and azaleas of which there are now extensive collections—in one area alone 260 different dwarf rhododendrons—but subsequently other ornamental trees such as acers, prunus, magnolias and birch have been added.

Garden open regularly (see Scotland's Garden Scheme guide and HHCG).

The Manor House, Bampton, Oxfordshire
The Earl and Countess of Donoughmore

When Lord and Lady Donoughmore came to the Manor House in 1982 they inherited an outstanding garden, created by Countess Munster after 1947, which had been severely damaged by the winter of 1981–2. Since then they have replaced many plants which were killed, while retaining as far as possible the structure of Lady Munster's garden. She built up the garden in the now well-established tradition of a series of enclosures, surrounded by walls or hedges and containing, for instance, a white garden and a rose garden. The Manor House is famous for the double herbaceous borders laid out and planted by Lady Munster, regarded by some as the 'best' borders in England. Many of the plants have had to be replaced by the Donoughmores. They have also made their own new additions to the garden such as extensive plantings of miniature daffodils and tulips under the lime avenue.

Garden open occasionally (see NGS).

The Manor House, Bledlow, Buckinghamshire
The Lord and Lady Carrington

The garden of the Manor House reveals the importance of beginning a garden by giving it a framework, in this case yew and beech hedges and pleached limes which have since 1948 grown to maturity. Within this structure the garden has steadily developed, its appearance strongly influenced by the unusually strong alkaline soil, around three sides of the striking house. Intimate and secret formal enclosures contrast with more traditional areas of herbaceous and shrub borders. *See pages 72–4.*

Garden open occasionally (see NGS) and by appointment.

The Manor House, Stanton Harcourt, Oxfordshire
Mr Crispin and the Hon. Mrs Gascoigne

The garden at Stanton Harcourt was created by William, second Viscount Harcourt and his second wife, Elizabeth, who came to live here in 1946—rather than return to the historic Harcourt family seat of Nuneham with its Brown landscape, later alterations by William Mason and William Sawtry Gilpin, and connections with William Robinson. Using the evocative setting of the medieval manor house, the church, Pope's tower and the old kitchen, and the series of ponds, stews and stretches of moat, Lord and Lady Harcourt planned a garden of two styles. Close to the buildings it has the atmosphere of a courtyard with formal paths and borders, while around the stretches of water it has an informal woodland atmosphere with lilac, philadelphus and viburnums beneath the older trees. In addition there are many urns and other ornaments, which Lord Harcourt brought from Nuneham and positioned with great skill at various vantage and focal points. Considering that most of the ponds were silted up when they started in 1948 and the areas of water and woodland garden a jungle of brambles it was an ambitious project. Lady Harcourt died in 1959 and since Lord Harcourt's death Stanton Harcourt has been the home of Mr and Mrs Gascoigne—his son-in-law and daughter.

Garden open regularly (see HHCG).

The Manor House, Walton-in-Gordano, Avon
Mr and Mrs Simon Wills

A garden of considerable horticultural interest only begun in 1976 when Mr and Mrs Wills bought the property. Fastigiate oaks along the drive are the first of many interesting and decorative trees they have planted throughout the garden. Closer to the eighteenth-century house are other trees, carefully grouped according to their characteristics, with spring bulbs such as erythroniums in the grass below. Warm borders on either side of the south-facing entrance front contain any plants collected by the Willses while travelling abroad, especially in the Mediterranean. The largest area of garden is concealed behind the house, where originally there was sloping lawn and rose beds. The roses have gone and the lawn closest to the house has been broken up by a series of new long beds containing a catholic mixture of small trees, shrubs, herbaceous plants and bulbs. Beyond an old tennis court has been transformed into a formal fragrant garden, enclosed by yew hedges and containing four square pools, flagged paths edged with lavender and an overall planting scheme of pink, blue and white. Along two sides raised beds contain many unusual alpines and other small plants, while on another is the Asian bank, containing only plants from that continent. Beyond here steps lead to an area of more informally planted standard trees including malus and other flowering varieties, purple Dawyck beech and *Davidia involucrata*. The garden contains the NCCPG National Collections of Cercis and Dodecatheon.

Garden open regularly (see NGS).

Marwood Hill, Barnstaple, Devon
Dr James Smart

Much of the twelve acres of Dr Smart's
garden is planted with trees and shrubs,
arranged in informal groups with grass paths
which can be kept rough-mown, in a manner
which characterizes many post-war gardens
of similarly extensive size and enables them
to be kept up with relatively low maintenance
input. The garden is on both sides of a valley
along the bottom of which the stream has
been dammed to form three lakes. Dr Smart
has gradually extended his planting down
the valley. The collections of many trees and
shrubs are outstanding: magnolias, birch,
sorbus and camellias for instance. Most interesting are the many, often extremely rare,
plants from Australia, New Zealand and Tasmania—many grown from seed collected by
Dr Smart on various expeditions; a represen-
tative variety of eucalyptus and a number of
more tender plants such as leptospernum are
among the Australasian visitors. A garden
which instantly reflects the passion for collecting and growing plants that has become
the primary source of enjoyment for
numerous modern gardeners. Dr Smart
estimates that the annual sale of plants in the
garden covers the wages of two full-time,
trained gardeners. *See pages 126–8.*

Garden open regularly (see NGS and
HHCG).

Mawley Hall, Cleobury Mortimer,
   Shropshire
Mr and Mrs Anthony Galliers-Pratt

Substantial restoration of the house during
the 1960s preceded the addition of gardens
designed both to be sympathetic to the
house's style and period and to blend
naturally in places into the surrounding parkland. The sunken rose garden was dug by
construction machines being used for work
on the house. As well as large quantities of
new trees, shrubs—in particular roses—and
spring bulbs, the most interesting addition is
the extensive herb garden, complete with
brick paths, stone statues and columnar
junipers. The herb garden connects the rose
garden with the swimming pool in front of
the delightfully converted stables.
See pages 143–4.

Garden open occasionally (see NGS).

Moseley Old Hall, Wolverhampton,
   Staffordshire
The National Trust

As at Little Moreton Hall, the National Trust
has added a carefully re-created garden at
Moseley Old Hall where no garden of interest
existed when it took on the property in 1962.
Originally Tudor, the house is most interesting for its connection with Charles II who hid
here after the Battle of Worcester. Therefore
the garden is seventeenth-century in inspiration. The main feature is an immaculate
parterre, containing a repeating pattern of
box-edged beds filled with gravel surrounding a central circular bed containing pebbles
and standard bay trees. The National Trust
has ensured that plants now in the garden
would have been in cultivation in the
seventeenth century—such as the *Clematis
viticella* and *Clematis flammula* on the wooden
arbour at one end of the parterre, the plants
in a small herb garden and fruit trees in the
traditional mixed orchard. If a reconstruction,
it is expertly done and undoubtedly gives the
house a new angle of interest.

Garden open regularly (see NGS and
HHCG).

Mottisfont Abbey, Romsey, Hampshire
The National Trust

The abbey itself was already surrounded by
extensive gardens, including a pleached lime
walk and other features added by Geoffrey
Jellicoe before the war, when the National
Trust acquired the property from Mrs Gilbert
Russell in 1957. The National Trust's most
notable addition has been away from the
house, in the old walled kitchen garden
where, since 1971, it has built up the most
comprehensive collection of old-fashioned
shrub and climbing roses in the country. The
rose garden was largely the brain-child of
Graham Stuart Thomas, at the time Gardens
Adviser to the National Trust. Thomas
designed the garden's lay-out and many of
the plants are those which he had been collecting together for many years previously.
He maintains that, 'there is at Mottisfont a
fairly complete picture of roses grown up to
about 1900'. The garden is given additional
interest by spring-flowering and late summer
herbaceous plants which have been added to
many of the borders. In a second walled

garden the National Trust has recently begun to build up a collection of shrub roses of Continental origin. The garden contains the NCCPG National Collection of pre-1900 shrub roses. *See page 56.*

Garden open regularly (see NGS and HHCG).

Nantclwyd Hall, Clwyd
Sir Philip and Lady Isabella Naylor-Leyland

Formal garden with pavilions, and landscape features and ornaments, designed and laid out by Sir Clough Williams-Ellis around the large house which he rebuilt extensively for the late Sir Vivyan Naylor-Leyland. Previously there were no gardens to speak of, only the marvellous parkland, which Williams-Ellis used to great advantage. *See pages 107–9.*

Okeover Hall, Ashbourne, Derbyshire
Sir Peter and Lady Walker-Okeover

Okeover Hall was substantially—and most successfully—rebuilt by Marshall Sisson for Sir Peter Walker-Okeover's father during the 1950s. Shortly after the house was completed the extensive surrounding gardens were given similarly thorough restoration and reconstruction. The new gardens were planned around the important existing features of the old walled garden and two long vistas planned in the eighteenth century, one to the west from the house's south terrace and the other away from the entrance forecourt, both terminating in eighteenth-century pavilions designed by Joseph Sanderson, the architect of the original eighteenth-century house. All the new planting in the garden, notably the pair of herbaceous borders flanking the walk leading to Sanderson's Temple of Pomona, was drawn up and supervised by Brenda Colvin, making Okeover particularly interesting as one of the few private gardens she worked on after the war. Statues in the garden were brought from the Victorian garden of nearby Osmaston Manor, another Walker-Okeover property where the house was demolished before work on Okeover was begun.

The Old Rectory, Burghfield, Berkshire
Mr and Mrs Ralph Merton

Mrs Merton has described herself as 'a green-fingered lunatic' and her garden, made since 1950, bears witness to her catholic love of plants and plantsmanship. Old-established and traditional varieties abound throughout, many of which have become quite uncommon in recent years. In addition there are other plants collected from abroad, for instance when the Mertons were travelling in Japan and China. As well as the quantity of plants which fill borders, sinks and other containers and cover the walls of the garden, house and outbuildings the garden has the strong framework of good design, notably the main vista of double borders leading from the house to a lake and statue at the far end. *See pages 81–2.*

Garden open occasionally (see NGS and HHCG) and by appointment.

The Old Rectory, Farnborough, Berkshire
Mr and Mrs Michael Todhunter

The delightful Queen Anne rectory provides the centrepiece for the garden made by Mrs Todhunter since she and her husband came here in 1965. The exposed position, high on the Berkshire Downs, affords enviable views but necessitates shelter by hedges to add to that provided by tall beech and lime trees. Old-fashioned roses and small-flowered clematis are outstanding in a garden full of interesting and well-chosen plants. The enclosed swimming pool garden, with its summer-house and luxuriant climbers is a spectacular surprise. *See pages 88–9.*

Garden open occasionally (see NGS).

Painshill Park, Surrey
The Painshill Park Trust

The recent restoration of the landscape at Painshill, created by Charles Hamilton between 1738 and 1773, rivals in importance that of its near-neighbour and contemporary, Claremont. Hamilton's garden was notable not only for its landscape and architectural features, some of which he designed himself, while others were by Robert Adam and Henry Keene. Unusually for the period, Hamilton also added a number of rare trees, in particular conifers, to the landscape. The restoration work has been painstakingly and expertly carried out and breathed new life into a unique chapter of English garden history. *See page 143.*

Garden open occasionally (see HHCG).

The Postern, Tonbridge, Kent
Mr and Mrs David Coaten

The Postern garden was made by Mr and Mrs Coaten's predecessor, John Phillimore, with considerable help from Anthony Pasley. It was begun during the 1950s and is an outstanding example of a modern garden with a formal design incorporating a series of different enclosures and more open areas, ambitious planting and fine Italian statues and other ornaments. Tall hedges provide shelter and intimacy and the structure is greatly enhanced by flights of steps and other architectural features constructed to a standard which has become a rarity in postwar gardens. The range of plants in the different parts of the garden is extensive, giving constant variety. Since coming to The Postern Mr and Mrs Coaten have maintained the high standards established by John Phillimore. *See pages 63–6.*

Garden open occasionally (see NGS).

The Priory, Kemerton, Worcestershire
Mr Peter and the Hon. Mrs Healing

Each of the different borders, which are the Priory's outstanding feature, reveals an overriding concern with balancing the individual colour, shape and foliage of different plants with the desired overall picture in a manner rarely seen in today's gardens. They reveal the considerable skill which has gone into the achievement of this balance. Also unusual is the almost exclusive use of herbaceous plants in these borders, with only occasional suitable annuals and shrubs being used to provide depth and height at the back. Quite different from the brilliant reds and oranges in one border are the pastel shades in the enclosed garden hidden away from immediate view. *See pages 130–1.*

Garden open occasionally (see NGS).

Pusey House, Faringdon, Oxfordshire
Mr and Mrs Michael Hornby

Mr and Mrs Hornby bought Pusey in the 1930s and before the war were preoccupied with removing a Victorian sunken rose garden and extensive shrubberies lying between the south front of the house and the lake, which was part of the original eighteenth-century landscape. At the same time they commissioned Geoffrey Jellicoe to design the broad terrace which now launches the imposing eighteenth-century stone house into its surroundings in a suitable grand and elegant manner. Beyond the terrace lie the wide expanse of the main lawn and uninterrupted views over the lake, with its eighteenth-century Chinese Chippendale bridge at one end and temple at the other, to the beech and other trees of the parkland beyond. On the far side of the lake they opened up the broad central vista, which had become completely obscured, with a wide swathe of grass between the flanking trees stretching to the distant boundary of a ha-ha. Since the war they have steadily clothed the twenty acres of garden with extensive planting, resisting the temptation to divide the garden with new enclosures and retaining its eighteenth-century spaciousness. One herbaceous border, one hundred yards long, curves in front of a brick wall to one side of the house, and double borders flank the central path in the walled garden. In addition to a water garden at one end of the lake they have cleared and replanted large areas of the shrubberies on both sides of the central vista, gloomy Victorian evergreens being replaced by more decorative and ornamental varieties and quantities of spring bulbs. A note of seclusion is found in the brick-walled privacy of Lady Emily's garden where a rich array of climbers surrounds beds of shrub roses.

Garden open regularly (see NGS and HHCG).

Rosemoor, Torrington, Devon
Lady Anne Palmer and Rosemoor Charitable Trust

Rosemoor is the garden of a collector. In the way in which its plants have been extensively supplied by seed or young plants from overseas, often collected in the wild by Lady Anne, it is a garden which continues a tradition established by many of the great gardens of the nineteenth and early twentieth centuries, but which has declined since the Second World War. The garden now contains a formidable array of plants, including many unusual and tender specimens—the latter mainly protected in warm sheltered spots beneath the walls of the house—growing in a variety of situations; long, sweeping, mixed borders, the large arboretum at one end of the garden, semi-woodland on the hillside along one edge, or in raised beds in the walled garden. Ornamental trees are perhaps the garden's main strength. Some varieties are grouped by family and the garden contains the NCCPG National Collection of Cornus. In 1987 Lady Anne Palmer donated the garden at Rosemoor to the Royal Horticultural Society. *See pages 128–30.*

Garden open regularly (see NGS and HHCG).

Saling Hall, Great Saling, Essex
Mr and Mrs Hugh Johnson

It is not surprising that the author of the hugely successful *International Book of Trees* should have made an arboretum the main new feature of his garden. Mr and Mrs Johnson bought Saling Hall in 1971 and his book was published two years later. The walled garden on one side of the house is largely as they inherited it from the previous owner, Lady Carlyle. The arboretum now contains a collection of many rare trees, some hardly ever seen in England. They are planted so as to divide the total area into a series of smaller ones, closely grouped trees providing screens and shelter. In different places there is a water garden, and a Japanese garden made where a steep bank had been dug in the past. It is a connoisseur's garden, for whom the trees, many of which have reached maturity, provide constant fascination.

Garden open occasionally (see NGS).

Shute House, Donhead St Mary, Wiltshire
Mr Michael and Lady Anne Tree

A highly imaginative garden made by the Trees since 1970 with the help of Geoffrey Jellicoe (who worked for Mr Tree's parents at Ditchley Park). The great feature is abundant water constantly bubbling out of the source of the River Nadder in the garden. The varying ways in which the water has been harnessed give the garden its highly individual character. Along one edge a still formal canal leads to low, classical Kentian grottoes and three stone figures on the bank above —copies of ones at Chiswick House. Very different is the rill where the water is constantly tumbling down the slope; first in a series of cascades between rich planting, and

below along a narrow channel running between formal pools with gravity-fed bubble fountains. Elsewhere the Trees have opened up a number of vistas across other ponds, focusing on well-positioned statues. Lady Anne has designed the main flower garden as a series of six large square beds, enclosed by box hedging and containing a mixture of flowers, fruit and vegetables. *See pages 49–50.*

Garden open occasionally (see NGS).

Stone Cottage, Hambleton, Rutland
John Codrington

Stone Cottage is a garden which would greatly appeal to today's plant conservationists and champions of our threatened native species. Not large, it reveals Mr Codrington's skill as a professional designer, which he has been for some years, and his extensive botanical knowledge. Beneath trees planted to give shelter and protection a feast of plants which once thrived in England's fields and woods grow and seed themselves freely in the old orchard where the grass is not cut until late summer, along winding stone paths, or in one area in a bed of gravel. In addition there are numerous plants which Mr Codrington has collected while travelling abroad, many of which thrive in the warm sun-catching garden in front of the house.

Garden open occasionally (see NGS) and by appointment.

Sutton Park, Sutton-on-the-Forest, North Yorkshire
Mrs Reginald Sheffield

Sutton Park is a striking example of a garden created to join an architecturally outstanding house to its parkland setting of equal quality. Mrs Sheffield and her late husband, Major Reginald Sheffield bought Sutton Park in 1962 and planned the garden themselves, with limited help from Percy Cane. The series of terraces, which descend from the house to the long beech hedge marking the boundary with the park, have both formality and grandeur which is ideally suitable, as well as the added interest of rich planting. From the lowest terrace wide lawns stretch out on either side to more informal groups of trees and shrubs and, on one side, a woodland walk notable for its flowering cherries and daffodils leads out into the park. Francis Johnson has recently designed an orangery

for Mrs Sheffield. *See pages 94–7.*
Garden open regularly (see HHCG).

Sutton Place, Guildford, Surrey
The Sutton Place Foundation

The gardens of Sutton Place are probably the most ambitious and certainly the most expensive to have been created in England in recent years. They were commissioned by Stanley Seegar, an American millionaire who bought Sutton Place in 1980 and who worked closely with the gardens' designer, Sir Geoffrey Jellicoe. For Jellicoe the work provided an opportunity to put into practice the humanist theories of landscape he had been evolving throughout his career. He planned the gardens, which revolve around the historic Tudor mansion taking in some of the features of existing gardens, as an allegory on human life. In a short period the scale of construction was spectacular. A twelve-acre lake was dug to the north of the house and 180,000 specially fired bricks, matching those of the house, were used to build the new east walled garden balancing the old one to the west of the house. For Jellicoe different parts of the gardens bear important relationships with modern abstract and surrealist painting. Stanley Seegar has now sold Sutton Place and parts of the original plan, such as the great cascade and grotto to the south of the house, sadly were never carried out. While the completed architectural features give the gardens a firm framework the planting, mostly devised by Lady Jellicoe, is still growing to maturity. Whether the gardens' development will see the expectation of their creation brought to fulfilment must now be uncertain. The great marble wall designed by Ben Nicholson will remain the most important piece of post-war English garden architecture. *See pages 50–3.*
Garden open occasionally.

Talbot Manor, Fincham, Norfolk
Maurice Mason

Talbot Manor characterizes to an unusual degree the delight of English gardeners in growing plants. It has steadily expanded since the war from limited areas around the house to its present size of thirty-five acres, and is now filled with an enormous range of plants. Its shape and appearance have steadily evolved as the garden has grown,
rather than being dictated by any overall design. In addition to the hundreds of plants in different areas of the garden, which represent virtually every group of plants hardy in this country, more tender varieties grow in a series of glasshouses.

Toddington Manor, Bedfordshire
Sir Neville and Lady Bowman-Shaw

The garden at Toddington Manor has been brought back from an advanced state of dereliction by the Bowman-Shaws since they moved to the house in 1979. With help from the professional designer Vernon Russell Smith they have built up a new garden around the limited features they found—notably the mature trees, old walls, a stream and various ponds. A path discovered during initial clearance is now a pleached lime walk running the length of the garden. The planting is mainly traditional, with old-fashioned roses, mixed borders and primroses and primulas in damper areas around the stream. The cost involved in creating a garden of five acres from virtually nothing has influenced the Bowman-Shaws' tendency towards well-known plants, rather than experimenting with what could be expensive—if more unusual—failures. This young garden already has a firm air of establishment. *See page 57.*

Garden open occasionally (see NGS).

Tremeer, St Tudy, Cornwall
Dr G.C. Haslam and Mrs C. Hopwood

Cornwall has become renowned for woodland-style gardens made by people interested in not only growing, but also breeding, plants—in particular, rhododendrons and camellias. The garden made at Tremeer by Major-General Eric Harrison between 1947 and 1978 is in this tradition. Camellias and rhododendrons predominate throughout the seven acres, including many specimens of blue or mauve rhododendrons, outstanding among the hybrids bred by General Harrison. His marriage to Roza Stevenson, who had previously built up an important collecton of rhododendrons with her first husband, further extended the quality of plants at Tremeer. *See pages 133–5.*

Garden open occasionally (see NGS) and by appointment.

Wadhurst Park, Sussex
Dr and Mrs H. Rausing

Wadhurst Park is one of the few modern country houses in England. Designed by the architect John Outram, it replaces a Victorian mansion on a superb site overlooking extensive parkland which falls away on all sides. The gardens are being designed by Anthony Pasley and are of unusual interest in their need to be sympathetic to the architecture of the new house. One striking feature is the Victorian winter garden which has been retained and restored at one end of the house and now contains hot and temperate conservatories. To one side of the house the old walled garden has been redesigned and planted. Large terraces extend along the two main garden fronts and on one side these drop away to woodland and water gardens which are still being cleared and planted.
See pages 59–60.

Westbury Court, Westbury-on-Severn,
  Gloucestershire
The National Trust

Westbury Court is one of the most important gardens to have been restored by the National Trust. It is an outstanding example of the formal late seventeenth- and early eighteenth-century gardens, strongly influenced by Dutch styles of the time and almost completely eliminated by the landscape movement. Since acquiring Westbury in 1967 the National Trust has effected a remarkable transformation of the garden, retaining the original features. The two silted-up canals were dredged, rebuilt and refilled, the pavilions taken down and rebuilt, hedges replanted and a formal parterre laid out to one side of the canals. In one corner a new small walled garden has been laid out containing traditional seventeenth-century plants and now Westbury has regained an appearance similar to the one it had when it was originally completed by its owner Maynard Colchester, around 1705.
See pages 141–3.

Garden open regularly (see HHCG).

West Green House, Hartley Wintney,
  Hampshire
The National Trust and the Lord McAlpine of
  West Green

Since becoming the National Trust tenant at West Green, a delightful red-brick house now restored after an extensive fire in 1982, Lord McAlpine has developed the garden in the tradition of eighteenth-century landscapists and folly-builders. Two new avenues have been planted, one of limes, the other of sweet chestnuts, leading out of the garden, the former to a tall fluted column of Portland stone. Like the other architectural ornaments which have been added to the garden, the column was designed by Quinlan Terry. It bears a Latin inscription whose translation reads, 'This monument was built with a large sum of money, which would have fallen, sooner or later, into the hands of the tax-gatherers.' The most individual folly in the garden is the classical Nymphaeum, with *trompe-l'œil* decoration, designed to be viewed through the circular Moon Gate cut into one of the brick walls of the old walled garden, from where flights of steps lead up to the Nymphaeum. Elsewhere a series of woodland walks surround a new lake and a wooden Chinese bridge crosses to an island where an ornamental aviary has been built.

Garden open regularly (see HHCG).

Woolton Farm, Canterbury, Kent
Sir James and Lady Mount

The garden at Woolton was largely planned and planted by Lady Mount's first husband, John Mount, during the 1950s and 1960s. Since his death she and her second husband, Sir James, who are both knowledgeable gardeners—he was knighted for his services to horticulture—have maintained the quality of plants and appearance in the garden which was an important priority for John Mount. The garden's mood suits perfectly that of the old farmhouse. Its main quality is skilful combination of foliage and flowering plants, notably a fine selection of ornamental trees, and spring and early summer flowering shrubs. These are contained in the series of large, flowing beds or as standards in the sweeps of lawn. Except in the small enclosed garden, with York stone paving, the curving lines of the design have great influence on the garden's understated character. The high standard of plantsmanship is evident in the conservatory which John Mount built, filled with half-hardy camellias and tender plants.

Garden open occasionally (see NGS).

SOURCE NOTES

CHAPTER 1

1 Miles Hadfield *Gardening in Britain* (1960). Republished as *A History of British Gardening* (1979)
2 Anne Scott-James *Sissinghurst: The Making of a Garden* (1975)
3 Harold Nicolson *Diaries and Letters 1939–45* (1967)
4 James Lees-Milne *Ancestral Voices* (1975)
5 E.V. Lucas *Over Bemerton's* (1908)
6 Harold Nicolson op. cit.
7 Anne Scott-James op. cit.
8 James Boswell *Life of Samuel Johnson*
9 Thos V. Hutchins *Priced Schedules* (1952, 1983)
10 *The Lyttelton Hart-Davis Letters* Vol. 2 (1978)

CHAPTER 2

1 Christopher Tunnard *Gardens in the Modern Landscape* (1938)
2 Sir Geoffrey Jellicoe *The Guelph Lectures on Landscape Design* (1983)
3 Sylvia Crowe *Garden Design* (1958)
4 J.C. Loudon *The Gardener's Magazine* (1832)
5 Miles Hadfield *Gardening in Britain* (1960)
6 Miles Hadfield etc. *British Gardeners. A Biographical Dictionary* (1980)
7 Miles Hadfield *Gardening in Britain* (1960)
8 Edward Hyams *The English Garden* (1964)
9 Harold Nicolson Introduction to *Great Gardens* by Peter Coats (1963)
10 Anne Scott-James *Sissinghurst: The Making of a Garden* (1975)
11 Miles Hadfield etc. *British Gardeners. A Biographical Dictionary* (1980)
12 Edward Hyams op. cit.

CHAPTER 3

1 Ex info. Sir Geoffrey Jellicoe
2 Brenda Colvin *Land and Landscape* (1948)
3 Michael Lancaster etc. *The Oxford Companion to Gardens* (1986)
4 Geoffrey Jellicoe (Editor) *Modern Private Gardens* (1968)
5 Evelyn Waugh *Diaries* (1976)
6 *Sutton Place* (Guidebook for Sutton Place Heritage Trust) (1983)
7 *Sutton Place* (1983)
8 Ex info. Sir Geoffrey Jellicoe

9 *Sutton Place* (1983)
10 *Sutton Place* (1983)
11 Ex info. Sir Geoffrey Jellicoe
12 *Sutton Place* (1983)
13 Russell Page *The Education of a Gardener* (1962)
14 John Sales *West Country Gardens* (1980)
15 *Country Life* (18 July 1985)
16 Ex info. Vernon Russell Smith
17 Ex info. James Russell
18 *Country Life* (14 May 1981)

CHAPTER 4

1 John Sales *West Country Gardens* (1980)
2 Ex info. Arthur Hellyer
3 Ex info. John Phillimore
4 *The Garden at Jenkyn Place* (Guidebook) (1986)
5 Ex info. Robert Adams
6 Alvilde Lees-Milne and Rosemary Verey *The Englishwoman's Garden* (1980)

CHAPTER 5

1 John Martin Robinson *The Latest Country Houses* (1984)
2 Alvilde Lees-Milne and Rosemary Verey *The Englishwoman's Garden* (1980)
3 Alvilde Lees-Milne and Rosemary Verey op. cit.
4 Alvilde Lees-Milne and Rosemary Verey op. cit.

CHAPTER 6

1 Sir George Sitwell *On the Making of Gardens* (1909)
2 Ex info. Lord de Ramsey
3 Ex info. Patricia Viscountess Boyd of Merton
4 Clough Williams-Ellis *Architect Errant* (1971)
5 John Martin Robinson *The Latest Country Houses* (1984)

CHAPTER 7

1 Edward Hyams *The English Garden* (1964)
2 Sylvia Crowe *Garden Design* (1958)
3 Edward Hyams op. cit.

CHAPTER 8

1 Sylvia Crowe *Garden Design* (1958)

2   Russell Page *The Education of a Gardener* (1962)
3   Miles Hadfield *A History of British Gardening* (1979)
4   Robert Pearson, etc. *The Ordnance Survey Guide to Gardens in Britain* (1986)
5   Ex info. Sir David and Lady Scott
6   Ex info. Sir David and Lady Scott
7   Ex info. Peter Healing

CHAPTER 9

1   Francis Bacon Essay *On Gardens* (1625)

2   Ex info. Marchioness of Salisbury
3   John Evelyn *Diaries*

CHAPTER 10

1   Ex info. Sir Geoffrey Jellicoe
2   John Sales, Foreword to *The National Trust, A Book of Gardening* by Penelope Hobhouse (1986)
3   Ex info. the National Council for the Conservation of Plants and Gardens
4   Christopher Brickell and Fay Sharman *The Vanishing Garden* (1986)

BIBLIOGRAPHICAL NOTES

The major part of the information for this book came from visits to gardens, and conversations with owners, professional designers and other individuals. In addition various editions of *Country Life* and the Royal Horticultural Society's journal, *The Garden*, were consulted for articles on specific gardens. Both publications have comprehensive indices of places featured in back editions. Purely factual information, particularly for the Gazetteer, came from the latest editions of the annual *Gardens of England and Wales* (the National Gardens Scheme guide) and *Historic Houses, Castles and Gardens in Great Britain and Ireland*. The *Bibliography of British Gardens* by Ray Desmond (St Paul's Bibliographies, 1984) provides invaluable guidance to source material on 5,500 gardens. The great majority of these are historic gardens, but a small number fall into the category of this book.

Quotations from various publications are listed among the various source notes. These include many of the books listed below which represent those most extensively consulted. They are divided into simple categories, with short comment, to illustrate their varying contents.

Guides and other books

The Gardens of Britain. (A series published by B.T. Batsford in association with the Royal Horticultural Society 1977–9, originally intended to cover Britain but eventually limited to six volumes: Devon and Cornwall; Dorset, Hampshire and the Isle of Wight; Berkshire, Oxfordshire, Buckinghamshire, Bedfordshire and Hertfordshire; Kent, East and West Sussex and Surrey; Yorkshire and Humberside; Derbyshire,

Leicestershire, Lincolnshire, Northamptonshire and Nottinghamshire.

Two similar volumes, *West Country Gardens* by John Sales and *West Midland Gardens* by Ron Sidwell were published by Alan Sutton in 1980 and 1981 respectively.

More selective, national, guides are *The Collins Book of British Gardens* by George Plumptre (Collins, 1985) and *The Ordnance Survey Guide to Gardens in Britain* (Ordnance Survey/Newnes/Country Life Books, 1986). *Garden Open Today* (Viking, 1987) contains short descriptions of 600 gardens which open for the National Gardens Scheme.

Private Gardens of England by Penelope Hobhouse (Weidenfeld and Nicolson, 1986) contains descriptions of 33 privately-owned gardens.

Gardens of the National Trust by Graham Stuart Thomas (Weidenfeld and Nicolson, 1979) contains descriptions of all National Trust gardens.

Garden History

For scholarship, breadth of content and readability, *Gardening in Britain* by Miles Hadfield is still unsurpassed. Originally published by Hutchinson in 1960 and reissued as *A History of British Gardening* in 1979 it is not out of date, but its coverage of the post-war years is limited.

A book of similar quality is *The English Garden* by Edward Hyams (Thames and Hudson, 1964) which traces the history of gardens through a selection created during different periods.

English Garden Design: History and Styles since 1650 by Tom Turner (Antique Collectors' Club, 1986) is a landscape architect's view of English garden history.

The Landscape of Man, Geoffrey and Susan Jellicoe's *magnum opus* published in 1975, goes far beyond just British garden history to discuss the evolution of the man-made landscape in which gardens play an important part.

Garden Design

Garden Design by Sylvia Crowe (Country Life Books, 1958) and *The Education of a Gardener* by Russell Page (Collins, 1962) are both acknowledged masterpieces by professional garden designers. *The Guelph Lectures on Landscape Design* by Geoffrey Jellicoe (University of Guelph, 1983) is somewhat more esoteric, but of considerable interest in cataloguing the English gardens where he has worked and putting forward his important views on landscape and garden design. Slightly dated, but a gem of garden writing, is *On The Making of Gardens* by Sir George Sitwell, published by John Murray in 1909.

General Information

British Gardeners, A Biographical Dictionary by Robert Harling, Miles Hadfield and Leonie Highton (A. Zwemmer Ltd in association with the Condé Nast Publications Ltd, 1980), is invaluable, pretty well comprehensive and contains far more than just notes on the leading personalities of British gardening.

The Oxford Companion to Gardens, Consultant Editors: Sir Geoffrey Jellicoe and Susan Jellicoe; Executive Editors: Patrick Goode and Michael Lancaster (Oxford University Press, 1986) is, as its title suggests, an important general reference book. Its style and contents are influenced by the fact that all the editors are landscape designers rather than garden historians.

Personal Memoirs, Histories, etc.

Gardens of a Golden Afternoon by Jane Brown (Allen Lane, 1982) describes the partnership between Gertrude Jekyll and Edwin Lutyens. *Wood and Garden* (Longmans Green, 1899) and *Home and Garden* (Longmans Green, 1900) are two of the many books written by Gertrude Jekyll herself.

Sissinghurst: The Making of a Garden by Anne Scott-James (Michael Joseph, 1975) gives an illuminating description from all angles of the famous garden, while *V. Sackville-West's Garden Book* (Michael Joseph, 1968) is a calendar of her writing taken from previous books, which all originally appeared in her column in the *Observer*. Her husband, Harold Nicolson, wrote three volumes of *Diaries and Letters*, all published by Weidenfeld and Nicolson.

Ancestral Voices, Prophesying Peace and *Caves of Ice* are three volumes of diaries by James Lees-Milne, covering the years 1940–7, all published by Chatto and Windus.

Conservation

The Vanishing Garden, A Conservation Guide to Garden Plants by Christopher Brickell and Fay Sharman (John Murray in association with the Royal Horticultural Society, 1986) is an important catalogue of plants in danger and begins with an historical assessment of the problem.

INDEX

(Note: *folio numbers in italics refer to illustrations*)